YOUR RIGHTS AT WORK

A

COMPREHENSIVE GUIDE
TO RIGHTS AT WORK
IN IRELAND

Eddie Higgins and Nuala Keher

© Institute of Public Administration 1994

ISBN 1 872002 42 0

Published by the Institute of Public Administration
57-61 Lansdowne Road
Dublin 4
Ireland

Typeset by: Peanntrónaic Teo
Printed by: Aston Colour Press

CONTENTS
Page

Foreword 1
Introduction: How to use the Book 3
Industrial relations procedures in Ireland 7

PART ONE
THE LEGISLATIVE ACTS 11

Summary of the Legislative Acts 13
Anti-Discrimination (Pay) Act 1974 17
Employment Agency Act 1971 21
Employment Appeals Tribunal 23
Employment Equality Act 1977 26
Holiday (Employees) Acts 1973, 1991 36
Industrial Relations Act 1990 41
Juries Act 1976 58
Maternity (Protection of Employees) Acts 1981, 1991 59
Minimum Notice and Terms of Employment Acts 1973–1991 65
Payment of Wages Act 1991 68
Pensions Act 1990 76
Protection of Employees (Employers' Insolvency)
    Acts, 1984–1991 82
Protection of Employment Act 1977 85
Protection of Young Persons (Employment) Act 1977 87
Redundancy Payments Acts 1967–1991 91
Safety, Health and Welfare at Work Act 1989 103
Safety in Industry Act 1980 106
Terms of Employment (Information) Act 1994 109
Unfair Dismissals Acts 1977–1993 115
Worker Participation (State Enterprises) Acts 1977–1993 126
Worker Protection (Regular Part-Time Employees) Act 1991 129

PART TWO
THE JOINT LABOUR COMMITTEES 135

Summary of the Joint Labour Committees 137
Aerated Waters and Wholesale Bottling Joint Labour
    Committee 140
Agricultural Workers Joint Labour Committee 144

Brush and Broom Joint Labour Committee   148
Catering Joint Labour Committee   152
Contract Cleaning (City and County of Dublin) Joint
    Labour Committee   160
Hairdressing (Cork) Joint Labour Committee   165
Hairdressing (Dublin, Dún Laoghaire and Bray) Joint
    Labour Committee   169
Handkerchief and Household Piece Goods Joint Labour
    Committee   174
Hotels Joint Labour Committee   178
Law Clerks Joint Labour Committee   183
Provender Milling Joint Labour Committee   187
Retail Grocery & Allied Trades Joint Labour Committee   190
Shirtmaking Joint Labour Committee   194
Tailoring Joint Labour Committee   199
Women's Clothing and Millinery Joint Labour Committee   205

Useful addresses and telephone numbers   211
Appendix: Code of Practice for the Employment of
    People with Disabilities in the Civil Service   218
Glossary of terms and abbreviations   220
Index   232

Foreword

As Minister for Labour Affairs, I am very much aware of how important it is for employers and employees to have ready access to information on our labour legislation so that they can fully understand their rights and obligations in this vital area. I therefore welcome this very practical guide which presents information on our labour laws in such a clear and straightforward manner.

Your Rights at Work covers more than twenty Acts and also deals with the legally binding minimum conditions of employment which are set down by sixteen Joint Labour Committees. This is a substantial block of legislative provisions and I compliment the authors on the production of a very readable and well indexed guide to what are, in many cases, quite detailed legislative instruments.

I agree with the authors' view that one of the main difficulties which many workers and employers have with labour legislation is the difficulty in attaining a clear understanding of rights and obligations. By making labour law more understandable *Your Rights at Work* makes its own important contribution to the achievement of fairness and mutual respect between employee and employer and thereby to industrial peace and job creation in the economy.

I have no doubt that this guide will prove to be an invaluable reference source not only for employers and employees but for all those involved or concerned with the area of rights at work.

Mary O'Rourke
Minister for Labour Affairs

INTRODUCTION: HOW TO USE THE BOOK

In a modern competitive economy, industrial peace is a prerequisite of wealth generation and job creation. It implies not simply the absence of strikes or disputes but rather the active presence of fairness and mutual respect between employee and employer and a willingness to adhere to the procedures governing the rights and obligations of people at work.

This approach to industrial peace is supported in Ireland by the legal provision of basic rights at work and through the co-operative efforts of the Department of Enterprise and Employment, the trade unions and employer organisations to establish a range of systems and services which support and improve industrial relations practice.

One of the consequences of increased legislation and more sophisticated procedures has been to make the practice of industrial relations more complex and therefore less accessible to many workers and employers. Our experience shows that far from having a clear understanding of rights and obligations, the most common questions asked by workers and employers when dealing with a problem at work are: What are my rights/ obligations in the matter? How do I exercise these rights or comply with these obligations?

Your Rights at Work sets out to answer those questions in a clear, friendly and direct manner. It does not pretend to be a word-for-word copy of various pieces of legislation or Employment Regulation Orders, but rather attempts to make the law itself and its structures and systems more readily understandable in terms of your rights and obligations at work.

In addition to the Legislative Acts and the Joint Labour Committees which are accessed through a comprehensive index, we have included a glossary of terms, a list of useful addresses, average rates of pay, and details of a significant civil service code of practice for the employment of people with disabilities.

Finally, some advice on dealing with problems at work. Despite the increasing complexity and sophistication of industrial relations, most disputes are resolved at a very early stage through discussion between those immediately involved. If at all possible, this is the best way to resolve problems.

Before you begin the process of raising a problem give it sufficient thought and consider all aspects, including the likely outcome of pursuing the matter. It is worth reflecting on the fact that exercising your rights can have negative as well as positive consequences.

Your Rights at Work is, of course, a secondary not a primary source so, in any serious dispute, or on any matter that could develop into a serious dispute, it is advisable, indeed essential, to consult with the experts, such as a trade union, the Department of Enterprise and Employment, the Employment Equality Agency, the Employment Appeals Tribunal, the Labour Relations Commission or the Labour Court. If, however, you decide to represent yourself you should acquire a copy of the relevant piece of legislation or a current Employment Regulation Order.

How to use the book: there are three paths into this book. If you are unfamiliar with a term, word, or concept you should consult the *Glossary*; if you are looking for a specific piece of information, and unsure where it may be, you should consult the *Index*; if your query concerns the provisions of a particular law or Joint Labour Committee, you should go to the *Table of Contents*.

Eddie Higgins and Nuala Keher
Doolin, County Clare
June 1994

Eddie Higgins has been a full-time trade union official since 1974. He has worked with the Workers Union of Ireland and with the Federated Workers Union of Ireland and is currently with the Services Industrial Professional Technical Union (SIPTU) in Galway.

Nuala Keher is the Adult and Continuing Education Office Project Manager in University College Galway, involved in training and education for community development organisations.

INDUSTRIAL RELATIONS PROCEDURES IN IRELAND

Industrial relations procedures in Ireland operate at a number of levels and a Labour Relations Commission Code of Practice issued by the Department of Enterprise and Employment covers this area. The main features are as follows:

Direct talks

These take place in the organisation or firm. They may involve you as an individual or as part of a group in discussions with your supervisor(s), manager(s) etc., with or without trade union representation.

Internal written procedures

Many companies have written procedures covering such matters as grievance, discipline, negotiation and consultation and these are used to structure the settlement of problems directly in the workplace. You should make a point of finding out what the procedures for resolving differences are in your firm or organisation.

Labour Relations Commission

Where it has been found impossible to settle a difference during direct talks and the internal procedures have been exhausted, it is usual to refer the dispute to a third party such as the Labour Relations Commission. The commission provides five services:

❏ Conciliation – an industrial relations officer attempts to find a settlement between the two parties through discussion and side-conferences.

❏ Rights Commissioner – generally hears cases involving individual claims or as the first stage in relation to certain rights, i.e. payment of wages, dismissal, maternity, contract information etc.

❏ Equality officer – investigates claims of discrimination at work on grounds of sex or marital status.

❏ Advisory service – aims to help employers and unions improve their industrial relations procedures and practices.

❏ Research and monitoring – ensuring that procedures are kept abreast of developments.

Joint Labour Committees

These are committees consisting of employer and union representatives under an independent chairperson which set minimum pay and conditions for specified occupations.

Joint Industrial Councils

These councils are established by employers and trade unions to set out legally binding pay rates, conditions and procedures in such areas as construction and state industrial employment etc. There are three registered Joint Industrial Councils. Their agreements are legally binding. There are eleven unregistered councils. Their agreements are not legally binding. The Labour Relations Commission services the councils.

Employment Appeals Tribunal

This tribunal hears cases regarding redundancy, minimum notice and terms of employment, dismissal, payment of wages, maternity etc. Its membership consists of an independent chairperson, legally trained, plus two ordinary members (one each from the employers and unions). If you are dissatisfied with a determination of the tribunal, the Circuit Court is the channel for further appeals.

| **The Labour Court** | Where the Labour Relations Commission decides that further conciliation is unlikely to resolve the problem, it may refer the case to the Labour Court. The court, in industrial relations terms, is seen as a court of final appeal. |

Normally the Labour Court relies on its moral authority and the voluntary attendance of the parties to a dispute but it can insist on attendance and has the necessary legal powers to do so in a number of areas, such as equality cases or cases of appeal against a Rights Commissioner's recommendation.

The Labour Court, by its own decision or at the request of the Minister for Enterprise and Employment, can intervene in a dispute and request the parties involved to attend a court hearing.

Labour Inspectorate

This is the enforcement agency of the Department of Enterprise and Employment and seeks to ensure that employers comply with minimum pay rates and conditions set down in the Employment Regulation Orders of the Joint Labour Committees.

Industrial action or strike action

All of the procedures outlined above are envisaged as pre-empting the need for strike action. In the event of a strike taking place, it is not unusual for any of the above stages to be used again in an attempt to settle the strike. The Labour Relations Commission or the Labour Court, therefore, may be involved in the same dispute more than once.

Employer Labour Conference

This is a national forum consisting of representatives of employers and unions and is used sparingly to resolve disputes.

Law courts   These are usually more formal than the procedures set out above and are generally not resorted to for solving industrial relations problems. Nonetheless, you can end up in a law court in certain circumstances, such as when appealing Employment Appeals Tribunal determinations or Labour Court determinations on cases regarding equality, industrial action or alleged breach of contract. In such cases you would normally be represented by a solicitor and/or a barrister.

PART
ONE

THE
LEGISLATIVE
ACTS

SUMMARY OF THE
LEGISLATIVE ACTS

Anti-Discrimination (Pay) Act 1974

To ensure that a woman and a man doing the same or like work, employed by the same or associated employers, in the same city, town or locality, obtain equal pay.

Employment Agency Act 1971

To provide for the regulation and control of employment agencies.

Employment Appeals Tribunal

To hear claims under the following Acts:

❏ Unfair Dismissals Acts 1977–1993
❏ Minimum Notice and Terms of Employment Acts 1973–1991
❏ Redundancy Payments Acts 1967–1991
❏ Protection of Employees (Employers' Insolvency) Acts 1984–1991
❏ Maternity (Protection of Employees) Acts 1981, 1991
❏ Worker Protection (Regular Part-Time Employees) Act 1991
❏ Payment of Wages Act 1991
❏ Terms of Employment (Information) Act 1994

Employment Equality Act 1977

To make it illegal to discriminate against a person on grounds of sex or marital status in respect of:

❏ recruitment
❏ conditions of employment other than pay
❏ provision of training or work experience
❏ promotion.

The Act is an attempt to stop employers favouring men above women or *vice versa* or favouring a single person over a married person or *vice versa*.

Holiday (Employees) Acts 1973, 1991	To ensure that workers are provided with paid leave.
Industrial Relations Act 1990	The Act covers two areas, trade disputes and industrial relations, its main aims being to:

❏ maintain and improve the framework in which industrial relations take place
❏ establish the Labour Relations Commission
❏ regulate certain aspects of trade union activity.

Juries Act 1976	To provide an employee with paid time off when called for jury duty.
Maternity (Protection of Employees) Acts 1981, 1991	To acknowledge two rights for women:

❏ the right to return to work after maternity leave
❏ the right to paid and unpaid maternity leave and to ante and post natal visits in accordance with the relevant social welfare Acts. There is no legal obligation under this Act on an employer to pay an employee during maternity leave.

Minimum Notice and Terms of Employment Acts 1973–1991	To provide a worker with notice of dismissal and with a legal right to written information regarding terms and conditions of employment.
Payment of Wages Act 1991	To provide a worker with a right to:

❏ an easily usable form of wage payment where cash is not being paid
❏ protection from unlawful deductions or

payments from wages

❑ a regular written statement of wages (pay slip).

Pensions Act 1990	To provide enhanced protection to a worker as a member of a pension scheme in respect of funding, trustees, disclosure of information and equality of treatment between men and women. The Act also established the Pensions Board which is responsible for ensuring that pension schemes comply with the legislation.
Protection of Employees (Employers' Insolvency) Acts 1984–1991	To provide an employee, in certain circumstances, with protection from pay-related losses when a company becomes insolvent.
Protection of Employment Act 1977	To provide earlier notification of, and information on, collective redundancies.
Protection of Young Persons (Employment) Act 1977	To provide young persons with protection on such matters as rest breaks, maximum hours, minimum age, employment records, night work and overtime.
Redundancy Payments Acts 1967–1991	To provide a worker with a lump sum payment, subject to certain conditions, on loss of job by reason of redundancy.
Safety, Health and Welfare at Work Act 1989	To extend legislative cover and to establish a National Authority for Occupational Safety and Health.
Safety in Industry Act 1980	To provide for the establishment of safety committees, delegates and representatives and to modernise the Factories Act 1955.

Terms of Employment (Information) Act 1994

To provide employees with a right to written information regarding their employment contract or relationship.

Unfair Dismissals Acts 1977–1993

To protect a worker against unfair or unreasonable dismissal.

Worker Participation (State Enterprises) Acts 1977–1993

To allow workers in certain state enterprises to elect directly from among the workforce up to one third of the membership of a particular board *and* to provide for sub-board level worker participation.

Worker Protection (Regular Part-Time Employees) Act 1991

To extend existing labour legislation to cover certain part-time workers.

ANTI-DISCRIMINATION (PAY) ACT 1974

Purpose

To ensure that a woman and a man doing the same or like work, employed by the same or associated employers, in the same city, town or locality, obtain equal pay.

Who is covered

All workers male and female. The Act works both ways.

DETAILS AND DEFINITIONS

Assessing your case

While the Act does not set out any procedure for you to evaluate your equal pay claim, the first step is to assess your work as against the work of the other person (of the opposite sex) on the basis of the definitions set out in 'Equal work' below.

If you believe you have a case, the options available to you are as follows:

❑ seek the advice of your trade union representative
❑ seek the advice of the Employment Equality Agency
❑ decide to represent yourself. This will involve a request to your employer to grant you equal pay.
If your employer rejects your claim, then you, or your representative, should refer your case to an equality officer of the Labour Relations Commission.

Associated employers

Where your equal pay claim is based on comparisons made with male employee(s) of an associated employer, the terms and conditions of employment must be common to you and the male employee with whom the comparison is being made.

Contracts

Your right to equal pay is in no way lessened where your contract of employment fails to refer to such a right.

Collective agreements

Collective agreements, registered employment agreements or employment regulation orders cannot discriminate in respect of pay rates on the basis of the sex of the employee.

Dismissal

It is unlawful for your employer to dismiss you solely or mainly because you decide to pursue a claim for equal pay. If this happens you are entitled to take a case for unfair dismissal to the Labour Court or a court of law, but not to both. This must normally be done *within six months* of the dismissal taking place unless the court is satisfied that the delay was reasonable and justified. The onus of proving that the dismissal was not related to your equal pay claim is on your employer.

Succeeding with your claim will mean either a cash award, the job back from a current date, the job back from the date of dismissal or a different job as may be decided.

Disputes

Your right to equal pay can be processed by you personally, by a trade union, or in certain circumstances by the Employment Equality Agency. The procedure is initiated through the equality officer and then, if necessary, the Labour Court.

Equal work

Equal work or 'like work', where the man and woman are employed by the same or associated employer in the same town, city or locality, is understood as follows:

❏ the woman is completely interchangeable with the man, *or*

❏ the two are doing the same job in the same conditions, *or*

❏ the jobs are more or less the same with any difference being either infrequent or of minor importance, taking into account the total job, *or*

❏ the jobs are performed in similar conditions and are of equal value in terms of skills, responsibility, mental and/or physical effort. Equal pay claims which arise in this situation will normally involve job evaluation.

Equality officer

If your employer has rejected your equal pay claim, the equality officer of the Labour Relations Commission will investigate your claim either at your request, at the request of your union or in certain circumstances at the request of the Employment Equality Agency.

Organising
the case

A statement of your case is sent to an equality officer who will forward it to your employer for comment. The employer's response will be communicated to you or to your representative by the equality officer. Normally twenty-one days are allowed for the submission to be supplied to the equality officer and a further twenty-one days for a response by the employer.

The equality officer will organise a conference of all concerned parties, which is held in private.

How the equality
officer works

The equality officer will attempt to ascertain the facts of your case through verbal and

19

written submissions (including job descriptions) and through cross examination by and of the parties involved.

As part of the investigation, the equality officer is entitled to seek and obtain the necessary information, to enter premises, to examine any relevant documents or records and to carry out a job evaluation.

Obstruction

Obstruction of an equality officer in the course of an investigation is an offence which can lead to a substantial fine being imposed on the person causing the difficulty.

Recommendation

The equality officer will, after the necessary period, issue a *recommendation.* The time period involved in the investigation, including the issuing of a recommendation, will vary depending on the complexity of the case.

Appeals

If you or your employer are dissatisfied with an equality officer's recommendation it can be appealed to the Labour Court but this must be done *within forty-two days* from date of issue.

Failure to implement a recommendation

If you suspect your employer is not going to implement an equality officer's recommendation you can appeal to the Labour Court. Do so *within the forty-two days* following the issuing of the recommendation. Having heard the appeal the court will issue a *determination.* The determination can be appealed by either you or your employer to the High Court on a point of law.

Failure to implement a determination or order	Should your employer fail to implement a determination, the Labour Court can issue an *order* to the employer. If the order is ignored, the employer, on conviction, can be fined on a continuous basis. In addition, the employer must pay compensation to you for loss of pay owing to the non-implementation of the Labour Court order.
Maximum retrospection	Winning your equal pay claim can mean up to three years' back pay plus keeping the higher rate of pay for the future.
Exclusions	The equality officer cannot hear cases of discrimination based on matters other than sex, for example race, creed, political belief.
Pay	This is called 'remuneration' in the Act and includes basic pay, holiday and sick pay, bonus, overtime, pensions, or any consideration in cash or kind which an employer gives to a worker directly or indirectly.

EMPLOYMENT AGENCY ACT 1971

Purpose	To provide for the regulation and control of employment agencies.
Who is covered	All employers engaged in the employment agency business and those workers who make use of them.

DETAILS AND DEFINITIONS

Dismissal
If you are dismissed by a contracted employer (the employer to whom you have been contracted), and this dismissal is found to be unfair in the terms of the Unfair Dismissals Amendment Act 1993, the employer rather than the agency will be liable, regardless of who is paying the wages or whether a contract exists between the agency and the contracted employer.

Fees
Fees *may not be charged* against you by an agency where the sole service provided to you is that of seeking employment for you.

Inspection
Inspection by authorised officers appointed by the minister is permitted. These officers are entitled to enter and inspect premises, and to seek and obtain any documents or records where they have reasonable cause to believe the Act is being contravened.

Licence
A licence from the Minister for Enterprise and Employment is required by any person wishing to operate an employment agency.

Licence revoked
This licence can be revoked where the minister is satisfied that the agency has committed an offence under the Act, has given false information, is not a suitable person, or operates from premises which are not suitable for the carrying out of this business.

Offences
Offences under this Act are punishable by fines which can be applied to directors, managers, secretaries etc. of the company concerned.

EMPLOYMENT APPEALS TRIBUNAL

Purpose

To hear claims under the following Acts:

❏ Unfair Dismissals Acts 1977–1993
❏ Minimum Notice and Terms of
Employment Acts 1973–1991
❏ Redundancy Payments Acts 1967–1991
❏ Protection of Employees (Employers'
Insolvency) Acts 1984–1991
❏ Maternity (Protection of Employees) Acts
1981, 1991
❏ Worker Protection (Regular Part-Time
Employees) Act 1991
❏ Payment of Wages Act 1991
❏ Terms of Employment (Information) Act
1994

DETAILS AND DEFINITIONS

**Employment
Appeals Tribunal**

The tribunal established by the Redundancy
Payments Act 1967 consists of:

❏ a chairperson and twenty-one vice-
chairpersons, all with legal qualifications
❏ a panel of forty ordinary members, twenty
nominated by the Irish Congress of Trade
Unions and twenty nominated by the
employer organisations
❏ a secretariat to assist the tribunal in the
discharge of its duties.

The Minister for Enterprise and Employment
is empowered to appoint additional vice-
chairpersons and/or ordinary members as
required.

Using the tribunal	If you believe you have a claim in respect of *dismissal, maternity, payment of wages or contract information* you can refer your claim to a Rights Commissioner. The outcome may be appealed to the Employment Appeals Tribunal *within six weeks.* In the case of dismissal, you have the further option of taking your case directly to the Employment Appeals Tribunal.

If your claim is about *minimum notice and terms of employment, redundancy* or *insolvency* you must go direct to the Employment Appeals Tribunal.

Specific forms must be completed when making a claim. These can be obtained from the Department of Enterprise and Employment, the tribunal itself or any FÁS office. |
| Organising the hearing | On receipt of a complaint the tribunal will advise your employer and provide an opportunity for a response. This response will be passed to you or your representative.

The tribunal will organise a time, date and venue for the hearing. There is usually a waiting period of at least three months but this can vary depending on the pressure of work on the tribunal. |
| Witnesses and records | You, or your representative, must notify any witnesses you are calling and in the event of it being necessary to force their attendance you must request the tribunal to issue a subpoena to you for serving on the witness. You must indemnify the tribunal against any costs that may be involved with regard to the subpoena. |

The tribunal is entitled to demand the presentation of documentation, records and related material. Requests to the tribunal for a subpoena to force the attendance of individuals or the presentation of documents etc. should be done as early as possible; such requests should state exactly who or what is required, and why.

Your employer is obliged to follow the same procedure described above when calling witnesses or seeking the presentation of documents.

Postponement

Postponement of a hearing is granted only where:

❏ there are critical circumstances
❏ seven days' notice is given to the tribunal before the date on which the hearing is due to take place, unless the tribunal decides for good reason to dispense with this requirement
❏ an individual appears and requests an adjournment
❏ the other party has at least been asked for its consent.

The granting of a postponement will, in all probability, mean your case will not be heard for at least a further three months or longer, depending on the pressure of work facing the tribunal.

Fines

Failure or refusal to attend, give evidence or produce documentation can lead to a fine of £1,000 per offence.

How the hearing works

The tribunal normally hears cases with the following in attendance: a chairperson or vice-chairperson and two ordinary members, one drawn from the employers' side, the other from the trade union side. In addition there is a secretary to each division of the tribunal.

The tribunal system of operation is to hear evidence from the parties through questioning, documentation etc. The tribunal can and does take evidence under oath.

The proceedings of the tribunal are normally held in public. On many occasions press reporters attend.

Outcome

A determination of the tribunal may be appealed to the Circuit Court *within six weeks* of its communication to the parties involved.

Powers of tribunal

The powers of the tribunal include:

❏ demanding and receiving any relevant documentation, records etc.
❏ summoning witnesses
❏ taking evidence under oath
❏ making decisions on the cases brought.

EMPLOYMENT EQUALITY ACT 1977

Purpose

To make it illegal to discriminate against a person on grounds of sex or marital status in respect of:

❏ recruitment
❏ conditions of employment other than pay
❏ provision of training or work experience
❏ promotion.

The Act is an attempt to stop employers favouring men above women or *vice versa* or favouring a single person over a married person or *vice versa*.

Who is covered

All employees, female and male, are covered under the Act, with the exceptions of:

❏ the Defence Forces, *or*
❏ where the sex of the employee is an essential qualification of the job, *or*
❏ where there are legal restrictions on the employment of a man or a woman in the particular post.

DETAILS AND DEFINITIONS

Advertising

Advertising of jobs in a discriminatory manner, e.g. the use of terms such as Barman, Busman, Salesgirl, is illegal. In addition those jobs which have traditionally been associated with one sex should carry a statement advising that applications from both sexes are welcome. A false statement made to secure the publication of a discriminatory advertisement can lead to prosecution of the person making such a statement. Magazines, newspapers, radio or television, as well as the employer who places the advertisement, are obliged to comply with the Act.

Complaints

Complaints regarding alleged discriminatory advertising are made by the Employment Equality Agency to the Labour Court. These are dealt with in the same manner as any other dispute referred to the Labour Court under this Act.

Fines

There is a liability of a £200 fine for breaches of this section by an advertiser who deliberately makes a false statement in order to get a discriminatory advertisement issued.

Agencies

Employment agencies which act as the middle person between the employer and the prospective employee cannot discriminate on the grounds of sex or marital status in respect of the services they provide. Employers may not give employment agencies instructions the implementation of which would discriminate on grounds of sex or marital status.

Civil Service and Local Authorities

The Civil Service and Local Appointments Commissioners must ensure that their application procedures do not discriminate on grounds of sex or marital status. However, the actual procedure of selection is outside the scope of this Act.

Collective agreements

Collective agreements or agreements between trade unions and employers, employment regulation orders or contracts of employment, sections of which may have discriminated on grounds of sex or marital status, became null and void when this Act was passed in 1971. The existence of such a contract or section of a contract does not affect a worker's right to protection from discrimination based on sex or marital status.

Compensation

Compensation *cannot exceed* an amount equal to two years' pay, excluding any financial benefit that might arise from the retrospective elimination of the act of discrimination.

Contracts

Contracts of employment, be they verbal or written, are deemed to include (whether in fact they do or not) a clause prohibiting discrimination on grounds of sex or marital status.

Direct discrimination

Direct discrimination is defined as treating a woman less favourably than a man because she is a woman or because of her marital status or *vice versa*.

Dismissal

It is unlawful for your employer to dismiss you solely or mainly because you decide to pursue an equality claim. If this happens you are entitled to take a case for unfair dismissal to the Labour Court or to a court of law, but not to both. This must normally be done within six months of the dismissal taking place, unless the court is satisfied that the delay was reasonable and justified. The onus of proving that the dismissal was unrelated to your equality claim rests on your employer.

Redundancy

In cases of dismissals arising from redundancy or disciplinary matters workers must not be treated differently on grounds of sex or marital status.

Employment Equality Agency

The agency, known as the EEA, was established under the Employment Equality Act. The EEA's function is to help make the legislation work. It has a major role in promoting equality of opportunity between men and women at work. It has a further responsibility to monitor the operation of equal pay legislation.

Special Powers	The EEA has the power to refer a case to the equality officer of the Labour Relations Commission where it believes that:

❏ discrimination is being generally practised
❏ your employer is in breach of the legislation
❏ it would be unreasonable for you to be expected to take the case on your own
❏ a person, through pressure or inducement, is attempting to force another person to discriminate.

Information	One of the EEA's most important functions is to advise and inform interested people about the Act and how it works.

Equality officers	If your employer has rejected your claim, the equality officer of the Labour Relations Commission will investigate it either at your request, at the request of your union or in certain circumstances at the request of the EEA. The initial request must be made to the Labour Court.

Organising the case	A statement of your case is sent to an equality officer who will forward it to your employer for comment. The employer's response will be communicated to you or to your representative by the equality officer. Normally each party is allowed twenty-one days to make or respond to a submission.

The equality officer will organise a conference of all concerned parties, which is held in private.

How the equality officer works	The equality officer will attempt to ascertain the facts through submissions, verbal and written, and through cross-examination by

and of the parties concerned. As part of the investigation, the equality officer is entitled to seek and get the necessary information, to enter premises and to examine relevant documents or records.

Obstruction	Obstruction of an equality officer in the course of an investigation is an offence which can lead to a substantial fine being imposed on the person causing the difficulty.
Outcome	The equality officer will, after the necessary period, issue a recommendation. This period will vary depending on the complexity of the case.
Appeals	If you or your employer are dissatisfied with an equality officer's recommendation it can be appealed to the Labour Court. This must be done *within forty-two days* from date of issue.
Failure to implement a recommendation	If you suspect your employer is not going to implement an equality officer's *recommendation* you can appeal to the Labour Court. You must do so *within the forty-two days* following the issuing of the recommendation. Having heard the appeal the court will issue a *determination*. The determination can be appealed by either you or your employer to the High Court on a point of law.
Failure to implement a determination or order	Should your employer fail to implement a determination, the Labour Court can issue an *order* to the employer. If the order is ignored, the employer can, on conviction, be fined on a continuous basis. In addition the employer must pay compensation to you for loss of pay owing to the non-implementation of the Labour Court order.

Winning	Winning your claim can mean receiving an amount up to, but not exceeding, two years' pay. Any financial benefit that might arise from the elimination of the act of discrimination is not included in calculating the two-year maximum.
Exclusions	Under this Act the equality officer cannot hear cases of discrimination which relate to pay or remuneration. These must be dealt with under the Anti-Discrimination (Pay) Act 1974.
Fair procedures	Where no significant difference between the work of the man or the woman or between that of the single person and the married person exists, it is illegal to discriminate on grounds of sex or marital status, in the following circumstances:

❏ selection for redundancy, short-time or lay-off
❏ allocation of holidays, overtime, shift work
❏ operation or application of any other work regulation, scheme (job evaluation, performance appraisal etc) or condition.

Favourable treatment	Favourable treatment awarded to a woman as a result of pregnancy or childbirth is not considered illegal under this Act.
Indirect discrimination	Indirect discrimination occurs where an employer demands that you comply with an employment requirement which is not necessary to the job and which is more easily complied with by a person of the opposite sex or different marital status.
Interview	Interview procedures must ensure that your sex or marital status are not used to your disadvantage.

| **Job offers** | Job offers must not discriminate on grounds of sex or marital status. For example, the same job cannot be offered to a married woman on terms which are less attractive than those offered to a single woman or man. |

| Refusal to offer a job | A refusal to offer a job because of the sex or marital status of the applicant is unlawful. |

| **Labour Court** | Use of the Labour Court or equality officers are the usual means of settling a discrimination claim where the employer has refused to concede the case (see also Labour Court under Industrial Relations Act 1990). |

| **Marital status** | Marital status cannot be used by an employer, employment agency, professional organisation, trade union or a training or education authority as a reason to treat you less favourably than another worker with a different marital status. For example, a single woman cannot be treated less favourably than a married woman simply because she is single and *vice versa.* |

| **Obstruction** | Obstruction of an equality officer is an offence which can lead to the imposition of a substantial fine. |

| **Occupational qualifications** | Qualifications which specifically require that a job be performed by a man or a woman are not unlawful under the Act where it can be shown in respect of each case that: |

❏ a man, or a woman, is required, for physiological reasons (e.g. acting or modelling), *or*
❏ no separate toilet or sleeping facilities exist *and* it would be unreasonable or impracticable for the employer to have to provide them, *or*

❏ members of both sexes are required to
carry out personal services for members of
their respective sexes, *or*
❏ the position involves travel and duties in a
foreign country where custom insists on
certain functions being carried out
exclusively by a man or a woman, *or*
❏ in the carrying out of certain duties within
the Gardaí or the prison service a man, or a
woman, is required.

**Positive
discrimination**

Positive discrimination is not unlawful where
the employer is attempting to address a
gender imbalance in a particular grade or
type of work. Such discrimination would
apply to special training programmes aimed
at introducing or increasing the number of
women in a particular area or level. You must
be able to show that in the previous twelve
months no women, or very few women, were
doing this work or were on the particular
grade.

Pregnancy

Any favourable treatment given to a woman
in respect of her pregnancy or childbirth is
not unlawful.

Pressure

Pressure to cause, maintain or hide
discrimination either by way of offers of
benefit or by threat is unlawful.

**Sexual
harassment**

While not specifically mentioned in the Act,
sexual harassment is nonetheless covered. If
you believe you have been sexually harassed
you can report the matter to the Labour Court
for investigation (see Equality officer).

Definition

Sexual harassment is defined by the
European Commission as 'unwanted conduct
of a sexual nature, or other conduct based on

sex affecting the dignity of women and men at work'.

This could include unwanted and/or repeated attention of a sexual nature, including physical, verbal or visual conduct. The person who believes he or she is being harassed is often the best judge of what constitutes harassment. There is an onus on your employer to take all reasonable stops to ensure that sexual harassment does not occur in the workplace. This includes advising employees that sexual harassment is unacceptable and may lead to disciplinary action up to and including dismissal. A 1994 court judgment has been made stating that an employer is not vicariously responsible for the actions of an employee, where the employer is unaware of sexual harassment taking place and where the employer does not condone the harassment. At the time of publication no appeal has been lodged against this judgment.

Time limit

You have six months from the date of the act of discrimination to make your claim. In other words, you must establish your claim *within six months* of the incident having taken place.

Escape clause

There is however an escape clause in relation to the six-month time limit, if you can show reasonable cause to the Labour Court for a delay in submitting your case. Talk to your union or the Employment Equality Agency.

Training

Work experience, opportunities for promotion and career guidance or advice must be provided in a way that does not cause discrimination on grounds of sex or marital status. Organisations such as national training authorities, FÁS and VECs are covered by the Act with regard to the courses they provide but only in respect of persons who are over the compulsory school-leaving age.

Unions

Unions or other worker, employer or professional organisations are covered by the Act and cannot therefore discriminate on grounds of sex or marital status with regard to the service they provide or in terms of whom they take into membership.

Victimisation

Victimisation for taking or having taken a claim, or for having participated in the proceedings of a claim under this Act is considered to be discrimination on the basis of sex, and therefore illegal.

HOLIDAY (EMPLOYEES) ACTS 1973–1991

Purpose

To provide workers with paid leave.

Who is covered
Annual leave

You are covered if you are over eighteen years of age and have worked for the same employer for at least 120 hours per month or 1,400 hours per year. If you are under eighteen the requirement is 110 hours per month or 1,300 hours per year.

NB Periods of illness are not included when calculating entitlement.

Part-time	You are covered as a part-time employee if you are normally expected to work for the same employer for at least eight hours per week and for at least thirteen weeks.
Public holidays	All employees are entitled to public holidays. If your employment terminates during the five weeks ending on the day before a public holiday and you have worked at least 120 hours during those five weeks you are entitled to that public holiday.

Public holiday entitlements are extended to day-to-day and part-time employees by the Worker Protection (Regular Part-Time Employees) Act 1991. |

DETAILS AND DEFINITIONS

Change of ownership	Where a change of ownership of the company takes place it does not affect your paid leave entitlement.
Church Holidays	Your employer may substitute the church holidays January 6th, August 15th, November 1st, December 8th, Ascension Thursday or Corpus Christi for a public holiday – except where they fall on a Sunday. In these circumstances you must be given at least fourteen days' notice. Neither St Patrick's Day nor Christmas Day can be substituted in this manner.
Disputes	If you have a dispute regarding your annual leave, calculation of holiday pay, timing of leave or any other matter, it can be dealt with by you, by your trade union, by the Minister for Enterprise and Employment or by the law courts.

Fines	If your employer fails to grant your annual leave or public holiday entitlement an offence is committed and the employer is liable to be fined.
Holidays	Your basic holiday entitlement is three weeks per year or proportionately less where you have been employed for under one year, e.g. 12 months = 3 weeks, 6 months = 1.5 weeks and so on. If you have worked for eight months or more you must be given two weeks' consecutive leave. If you are a regular part-time employee as defined in the Worker Protection (Regular Part-Time Employees) Act 1991 you are entitled to annual leave at the rate of six hours' paid leave for every hundred hours worked.
Minimum leave	Minimum leave entitlements are set out in the Act but many employees, particularly members of trade unions, have in excess of these amounts, i.e. nineteen to twenty-two days per year in addition to public holiday entitlement.
Pay	Pay for annual leave must be paid *in advance* of going on holidays.
Method of calculation	Pay for annual leave should be calculated as follows, noting that *overtime payments are excluded* from the calculation: ❑ For those workers on a fixed basic pay rate (hourly, weekly, fortnightly or monthly): basic rate plus any additional regular payment, bonus or allowance which does not change by reference to work done (quotas) ❑ For all other workers: basic weekly rate arrived at by dividing the thirteen weeks' earnings prior to the leave period by thirteen

and multiplying the result by the number of weeks' leave to be taken.

Board and lodging
If your weekly wages are reduced to take into account board and/or lodgings this amount must be included when calculating holiday pay.

Payment in lieu
Payment in lieu should be made if holidays are owed to you when you are leaving employment. This is calculated on the basis of 25 per cent of your weekly pay for each month worked for the employer.

Public holidays
Public holidays are often mistaken for bank holidays. Remember, you have a legal right to a public holiday but no such right exists for bank holidays unless of course you work in a bank. For example, Good Friday is a bank holiday. It is not a public holiday.

Public holidays are as follows:

January 1 (New Year's Day)
March 17 (St Patrick's Day)
Easter Monday
First Monday in May
First Monday in June
First Monday in August
Last Monday in October
Christmas Day
St Stephen's Day

If New Year's Day, St Patrick's Day or St Stephen's Day fall on a weekend then the next Monday is given for the holiday. If Christmas Day falls on a weekend then the following Tuesday is given as the holiday. Where New Year's Day, St Patrick's Day or St Stephen's Day fall on a Saturday, it is practice to grant an additional day's leave, though not specified in the Act.

Public holiday entitlement

You are entitled to any one of the following alternatives as decided by the employer:

❑ a paid day off on the holiday itself
❑ a paid day off within a month
❑ an extra day's annual leave
❑ an extra day's pay.

Sickness

Certified sickness when on annual leave means you are not considered to be on leave and the period must be allowed to you again. For example, if you are on a fortnight's holiday, and you become sick at the start of the second week, you are owed a week's leave. You do not, however, get paid twice for the annual leave period.

Effect on entitlement

Time spent out sick cannot be included in calculating your annual leave entitlement.

Timing of leave

The employer decides when you can take your leave but either you or your union must be consulted at least one month beforehand. Due regard must be had to your right to rest and recreation. Leave must be taken within the leave year (1 April – 31 March) or within six months of its completion.

INDUSTRIAL RELATIONS ACT 1990

Purpose

The Act covers two areas, trade disputes and industrial relations, its main aims being to:

❏ maintain and improve the framework in which industrial relations take place
❏ establish the Labour Relations Commission
❏ regulate certain aspects of trade union activity.

Who is covered

For the purposes of *trade disputes* (strikes, industrial action etc.) all workers other than members of the Gardaí and Defence Forces.

For the purposes of *industrial relations* all workers with the exception of:

❏ state employees
❏ teachers (first and second levels)
❏ local authority officers
❏ health board officers
❏ vocational education officers and school attendance committee officers.

DETAILS AND DEFINITIONS

Associated Acts

Acts which are associated with this piece of legislation include the following:

❏ Conspiracy and Protection of Property Act 1875
❏ Trade Disputes Act 1906 and Amendment 1982
❏ Trade Union Acts 1941, 1971
❏ Industrial Relations Acts 1946, 1969, 1976.

Codes of practice

These consist of guidelines for the social partners on a range of industrial relations matters. The social partners include government, employer, farmer and trade union representation. Codes of practice are prepared by the Labour Relations Commission, normally in consultation with the social partners, and then submitted to the Minister for Enterprise and Employment for consideration.

Implications
of the codes

It is important to note that once the minister issues a code of practice it shall be taken into account by the Labour Court, Labour Relations Commission, law courts, Employment Appeals Tribunal etc. in deciding on particular issues. The main objective of these codes is the promotion of good industrial relations practice.
Codes of practice are not legally binding. The Labour Court may interpret a code or investigate an alleged breach of a code where the Labour Relations Commission has so agreed.

Two codes of practice have been issued. These cover employee representatives (1993) and dispute procedures generally and in essential services (1992) as follows:

Duties and Responsibilities of Employee Representatives and the Protection and Facilities to be afforded to them by their Employer (1993)

Who is
covered

Those covered include employee representatives, shop stewards, staff representatives etc. who:

❏ are elected or designated in accordance with the rules of their representative organisation
❏ abide by their own representative organisation's regulations, *and*
❏ abide by agreements made between their representative organisation, e.g. trade union, and their employer.

Protections

Such employees should be afforded certain protections and facilities. They should not, because of their representative position or their representative activities, be dismissed, receive unfair treatment, be unfairly selected for redundancy, have their conditions changed unfavourably or be made to endure any action threatening their security of employment.

Before any action is taken against a representative the relevant union must be consulted by the management.

Facilities

Bearing in mind the size and capabilities of the enterprise or organisation and without unduly interfering with its safe and efficient operation the employee representative should, in a reasonable manner, be afforded the following facilities:

access to
❏ the relevant management
❏ the various parts of the workplace

paid time off during working hours
❏ for representative duties
❏ for attending trade union courses
❏ to collect union dues
❏ to communicate with the membership through the use of notice boards or the

distribution of non-political news sheets, magazines etc.

The prior permission of the management is needed for all these facilities.

Dispute Procedures including Procedures in Essential Services (1992)

Who is
covered

Workers and employees generally but particularly those involved in essential services.

Procedures

The procedures should be as comprehensive as possible. They should be in writing, and be made known to the employees.
They should provide for the referral of disputes to the Labour Relations Commission, the Labour Court or any other mutually agreed third party on the understanding that both parties have in the first instance made every effort to secure a settlement without recourse to outside agencies.
Procedures should prohibit any action by either party which would:

❏ interfere with the smooth operation of the procedures
❏ be designed to bring pressure to bear on the other party where the procedures are being honoured
❏ take place before the exhaustion of the procedures
❏ take place before seven days' notice of action had been given, where the procedures had been exhausted (or any longer period of notice agreed between the parties).

Emergency and minimum services	Where, despite the efforts of all parties, a dispute takes place it is in the common interest of union and employer to ensure minimal damage. Both parties should therefore enter into arrangements for the maintenance of plant, machinery, process, or the provision of medical services or emergency services on humanitarian grounds and the necessary precautions regarding safety, health and security.
Essential services	These are defined as including those services which if affected by an industrial dispute could:

❏ endanger life
❏ cause major damage to the national economy or
❏ cause widespread hardship to the community.

Particular attention is focused on the health services, energy supplies, water and sewerage services, ambulance, fire and other rescue services, air traffic control and other elements of public transport. This list is not intended to be comprehensive.

Special procedures for essential services	In order to limit the likelihood of industrial action the parties are requested to enter into special arrangements which include the following options:

❏ the parties may agree to accept the outcome of the final stage of their dispute procedures, i.e. the findings of the Labour Court, of the agreed arbitration board or tribunal or independent person appointed by both parties, *or*
❏ should either party indicate that the

outcome, from the final stage of their disputes procedure, as outlined above, is not satisfactory then the parties may agree a means of resolving the issue without a strike or other form of industrial action. Such an agreement would include a provision for a review of the case within twelve months. The outcome of this review would be binding on both parties.

Keeping the peace in essential services

Where there is a real or perceived threat to continued essential supplies or services then the Irish Congress of Trade Unions and the Irish Business and Employers Confederation should be consulted by the Labour Relations Commission provided it is satisfied that all available procedures have been used.
The purpose of this consultation is to secure the co-operation of both organisations so that normal work may proceed for a period of no longer than six months. During this time further efforts would be made to resolve the dispute.

Conciliation conferences

Conciliation conferences of the Labour Relations Commission take place when negotiations at company level have failed to resolve a workplace problem. A conciliation conference is requested by either an employer or a union or by the commission itself.

Exclusions

❏ A conciliation conference can take place only with the agreement of both parties to the dispute.
❏ The conciliation service cannot deal with equality cases, i.e. discrimination based on sex or marital status. Such cases are handled by the equality officers of the Labour Relations Commission.

❑ Cases which have had a full hearing by the Labour Court are not usually the subject of conciliation conferences.

❑ Where unofficial industrial action is continuing the conciliation service will not normally become involved.

❑ Where a Rights Commissioner has issued a recommendation on the matter in dispute a conciliation conference cannot be held.

Organising the conference

The Labour Relations Commission will organise a conciliation conference on its own initiative or at the request of either party to the dispute. The commission assigns an industrial relations officer (also known as a conciliation officer) to the case and s/he will organise the date, time, venue etc. of the conciliation conference.

Conciliation conferences are held in private.

How the conference works

At the conference the conciliation officer asks both sides to give a brief statement of the problem.

Having heard both sides and clarified any matters arising the conciliation officer breaks the parties into two side-conferences. In the privacy of these side-conferences the conciliation officer will attempt to find a solution or compromise acceptable to both parties.

Outcome

The conclusion of the conference is reached by settlement, adjournment, referral back to local level for further discussion, referral to the Labour Court for a full hearing, or to a Rights Commissioner, or other appropriate third party.

Disputes

Workers who are in dispute with one another but not with their employer, and whose dispute affects their work, are not immune from lawsuits by the employer for loss of trade or from charges of criminal conspiracy.

Employer

'Employer' means someone who employs you, did employ you or seeks to re-employ you either alone or along with other people.

Immunity from prosecution

Immunities provided to authorised trade unions and their members who, following a proper secret ballot, are involved in industrial action which aims to alter or maintain a contract of employment include:

❏ freedom from prosecution for interfering with trade or business
❏ freedom from prosecution for breach of contract
❏ freedom from prosecution for getting someone else to breach their contract of employment.

These immunities *are granted* to members of an authorised trade union involved in industrial action and *are not granted* to non-members similarly involved in a dispute with their employer.

Individual grievance

If the immunities under the Act are to apply to industrial action taken in support of a grievance affecting only one individual, the grievance must have been handled in accordance with the agreed procedures in your organisation, be they written or established through custom and practice, before industrial action can be taken. Otherwise you are not protected from prosecution.

Industrial action   Industrial action is defined as any action taken by an individual worker or group of workers which is aimed at forcing an employer to change or maintain their contract of employment (be it written or verbal) in regard to pay, holidays, work practice, hours, pensions etc. Industrial action is taken to include overtime bans, work-to-rules, go-slows, stoppages etc., as well as strikes.

The common legal understanding of an industrial action is any action taken 'in contemplation of or in furtherance of a trade dispute'.

Injunctions   Injunctions are sought as a means of preventing or frustrating industrial action. They may not be granted by the courts where:

❏ in the case of an *ex parte* injunction (i.e. where one of the parties to the dispute is not present when the application for an injunction is made) when
• a proper secret ballot was held, *and*
• at least one week's notice of intention to take industrial action was given to the employer, *and*
• no damage to property, trespass, occupation of premises, loss of life or personal injury has occurred
❏ in the case of an *interlocutory* injunction (i.e. where both parties are present when the application for an injunction is made) when
• all of the conditions attaching to a refusal to grant an *ex parte* injunction apply, *and*
• you or your trade union can establish a fair case that a trade dispute is involved.

Joint Industrial Councils

There are three registered Joint Industrial Councils:

❏ Footwear Industry
❏ Dublin Wholesale Fruit and Vegetable Trade
❏ Construction Industry

Apart from the three registered Joint Industrial Councils there are eleven unregistered councils:

❏ Bacon Curing
❏ Bakery and Confectionery Trade
❏ Banks
❏ Electrical Contracting Industry
❏ Flour Milling
❏ Grocery Provision and Allied Trades
❏ Hosiery and Knitted Garments Manufacture
❏ Printing and Allied Trades in Dublin
❏ State Industrial Employees
❏ Woollen and Worsted Manufacture
❏ Telecom

For further information you should contact the Labour Relations Commission.

Joint Labour Committees

These committees establish minimum rates of pay and conditions of employment for certain categories of workers (see separate section on Joint Labour Committees).

Labour Court

The Labour Court, in industrial relations terms, is the court of final appeal. In most cases the court draws its authority from the voluntary participation of the parties involved in disputes. In other circumstances it can compel participation such as in equality cases or cases of appeal against a

Rights Commissioner's recommendation. It currently consists of three divisions.

Each division of the Labour Court consists of three persons appointed by the Minister for Enterprise and Employment, namely a chairperson or vice-chairperson and two ordinary members of the court, one appointed on the recommendation of the Irish Business and Employers Confederation (IBEC) and one on the recommendation of the Irish Congress of Trade Unions (ICTU).

Organising the hearing

The Labour Court will investigate disputes in any of the following situations:

❏ the Labour Relations Commission decides, with the agreement of the parties, to refer the dispute to a full hearing of the court
❏ the commission decides to waive its conciliation function
❏ the Minister for Enterprise and Employment requests the court to intervene in a dispute, *or*
❏ the case is taken under the Anti-Discrimination (Pay) Act 1974 or the Employment Equality Act 1977
❏ there are appeals arising from a Rights Commissioner's investigations.

The court will normally advise the parties in writing of the date, time and venue of the hearing. Written submissions must be received by the court three working days before the hearing takes place.

How the hearing works

Though less formal than a court of law you are nonetheless expected to stand when the court members enter. Smoking is not allowed during the proceedings.

The Labour Court normally operates on the basis of written submissions, usually exchanged between the parties at the time of the hearing, which are then read in court by the parties concerned, followed by:

❑ verbal argument
❑ cross-examination.

Outcome

The Labour Court will issue its findings in due course. These findings can take the form of a recommendation, an arbitration finding, a determination or a decision.

Recommendation

A recommendation is not binding on either party but carries the moral authority of the Labour Court.

Arbitration finding

❑ Under Section 20 of the 1969 Industrial Relations Act an arbitration finding is binding on both parties where they agree to this prior to the hearing. Where the dispute was referred by the union to the Labour Court against the wishes of the employer, the Labour Court is entitled to hear the case *with or without the presence of the employer;* but the union must agree in advance to accept the findings of the court. It is not binding on the employer.

Determination

A determination results from an appeal to the Labour Court taken under the equality legislation where you seek the implementation of an equality officer's recommendation, or either you, or your employer, appeal against an equality officer's recommendation. Such determinations by the Labour Court can be appealed to the law courts only on a point of law.

Decision	An appeal against a Rights Commissioner's recommendation results in a decision being made by the Labour Court under the Industrial Relations Act 1969. The Labour Court's decision in this case is final.
Labour Relations Commission	The commission was established under the Industrial Relations Act 1990 to maintain and improve the framework and practice of industrial relations, through the provision of the following services:

❏ an advisory service to identify and resolve underlying difficulties which are a cause of on-going industrial relations unrest
❏ conciliation, equality and Rights Commissioners' services
❏ research and monitoring of industrial relations developments and machinery
❏ preparation of codes of practice
❏ assistance to Joint Labour Committees and joint industrial councils.

The commission consists of a chairperson, plus six ordinary commission members. Two members are nominated by the Irish Business and Employers Confederation (IBEC), two by the Irish Congress of Trade Unions (ICTU) and two by the Minister for Enterprise and Employment, who appoints all six.

Picketing

Picketing against your employer must, where practical, be at your place of employment, or where not, at its approaches. It is legal as long as:

❏ it is peaceful
❏ it is only for the purpose of getting and giving information about the strike

❏ it is used as a peaceful attempt to convince other people to support the strike.
It is not lawful to picket your employer's home unless it can be demonstrated that the business is being carried on from that address.

Secondary picketing

Pickets may also lawfully be placed on employments other than your own where you could reasonably believe that the other employer was acting to weaken your strike, unless the actions in question are life-saving and the employer is involved in an essential service.

Who can picket

Only those employees in dispute, and union officials, may picket at your place of employment.

Registered Employment Agreements

Registered employment agreements which provide legal minimum wage rates and conditions of employment for certain workers are enforceable under this Act and breaches can lead to the employer's being fined and any outstanding monies being paid to the employee.

Rights Commissioners

Rights Commissioners are appointed by the Minister for Enterprise and Employment to investigate cases normally involving an individual employee. Investigations generally take place only with the agreement of both parties.

Exclusions

The Rights Commissioner will not normally investigate cases:

❏ which involve groups of workers, *or*
❏ where the matter has already been the subject of a Labour Court investigation, *or*

❑ where either of the parties to the dispute has objected in writing to the case being heard by the Rights Commissioner. The Rights Commissioner must be advised of the objection to the hearing *within three weeks* of the notice of the intention to investigate a matter/dispute.

Organising the case	A Rights Commissioner's investigation normally proceeds as follows:

❑ A request for a dispute to be investigated is made in writing or by telephone (but which must later be confirmed in writing) by an employer, a union or an individual.
❑ The Rights Commissioner will contact both parties, in writing, to ascertain if they are agreeable to the investigation's going ahead. If either side objects within three weeks of receipt of notification of the investigation then the case cannot be heard by the Rights Commissioner *unless* it has been referred under the Unfair Dismissals Acts, the Payment of Wages Act or the Terms of Employment (Information) Act, in which case the employer is obliged to attend.

How the conference works	When the investigation takes place the parties normally produce written submissions detailing the problem(s) and the main arguments for their respective positions. Verbal submissions and cross-examination by the Rights Commissioner and the parties involved ensues.
Outcome	Following the investigation the Rights Commissioner will issue a recommendation in due course (normally ten days). However, it may also happen that the case can be settled prior to the issue of a recommendation.

Appeals	Appeals against a Rights Commissioner's recommendation must be made in writing to the Labour Court or Employment Appeals Tribunal *within six weeks* of the date of the recommendation. A decision of the Labour Court on an appeal against a Rights Commissioner's recommendation *is final and binding on all parties* whilst that of the Employment Appeals Tribunal may be appealed to the High Court on a point of law.
Secret ballots	For authorised trade unions to enjoy the immunities provided by the Act a proper secret ballot on the question of taking industrial action or strike action must be held. It must meet the following criteria:
Proper ballot	❏ the governing body of the union must maintain control over all aspects of the ballot and its consequences ❏ it must take place before the commencement of industrial action or before supporting industrial action is taken by another union ❏ when it is taking place, it must include all the members the union reasonably believes will be involved in the forthcoming industrial action ❏ the results must be made known to the members concerned as soon as is practical after the vote has concluded.
Changing the result	The results of a ballot against industrial action may be overturned by the governing body of a trade union. This may be done only in a combined or aggregate vote with other unions, where the overall result is in favour of taking industrial action.

Unofficial action	Trade unions are prohibited from participation in any way in strikes or industrial action which have not been preceded by a proper secret ballot.
Right of appeal	If, as a member of a trade union, you believe a secret ballot vote in your union has not been conducted properly, you have the right of appeal either within the union or through the law courts. This right does not extend to an employer.
Trade dispute	'Trade dispute' is defined as a dispute between worker(s) and an employer(s) concerning, or likely to affect, terms or conditions of employment or non-employment. The term does not cover disputes between workers where immunity from prosecution does not apply.
Trade union rules	Trade union rules preclude union involvement in any way with a strike or any form of industrial action which has not been preceded by a proper secret ballot.
Worker	A 'worker' is defined as someone who was, or is, in the employ of an employer, with the exception of members of the Defence Forces and the Gardaí.
Worker v. Worker disputes	Where you are involved in a dispute with a colleague worker and your employer does not take sides, you do not have immunity from prosecution should you take industrial action.

JURIES ACT 1976

Purpose
To provide an employee with paid time off when called for jury duty.

Who is covered
Those aged between eighteen and seventy years.

DETAILS AND DEFINITIONS

Exceptions
Those who can be excused, disallowed or debarred, as appropriate, from jury duty include:

❏ teachers, doctors, nurses, paramedics, students, nuns, priests, mullahs, monks, rabbis, TDs, senators, soldiers
❏ persons aged between sixty-four and seventy years
❏ convicts
❏ people who have served on a jury in the three years prior to the current summons
❏ disabled persons
❏ people suffering from mental infirmities.

Failure to attend
Failure to attend for jury duty could mean your being fined unless you have good reason.

Holiday
Your holiday entitlement continues to be earned while you are on jury duty.

Payment of wages
When you are on jury duty you are considered to be at work and your employer is obliged to pay you your salary. Failure to do so can be brought to the attention of the law courts and could result in the employer's being fined.

Service

Your service with the company is unbroken by jury duty for the purposes of calculating entitlement under redundancy, minimum notice, unfair dismissal, and part-time workers legislation.

MATERNITY (PROTECTION OF EMPLOYEES) ACTS 1981, 1991

Purpose

To acknowledge two rights for women:

❏ the right to return to work after maternity leave
❏ the right to paid and unpaid maternity leave in accordance with the relevant social welfare Acts and attendance at antenatal and post-natal appointments. There is no legal obligation under this Act on an employer to pay an employee during maternity leave.

Who is covered

Any employee who works for more than eight hours per week and for at least thirteen weeks for the same employer, or an employee who is on a fixed-term contract which has at least twenty-six weeks left to run.

DETAILS AND DEFINITIONS

Alternative work

Suitable alternative work can be offered by the employer to you on your return from maternity leave if it is unreasonable or impractical to give you back your old job. In these circumstances the new job cannot be significantly less in terms of pay, grade, hours, leave etc. than your post prior to maternity leave.

Ante/Post-natal visits during working hours are allowed for under the Act as follows:

Antenatal
Any number of visits for any length of time subject to their being under the supervision of a registered medical practitioner. Two weeks' written notice must be given to the employer. From October 1994 you are entitled to paid time off where such visits have to take place during working hours.

Post-natal
Post-natal visit(s) must occur within fourteen weeks of the birth. Two weeks' written notice of each visit must be given to the employer.

Proof of visits
If your employer requests written proof of the visit(s) you must provide it.

Medical emergency
If, for good reason, e.g. medical emergency, you cannot give the required notice, you still have the right to antenatal visits provided you can produce written proof within one week of having attended for antenatal care.

Still birth
In the case of a still birth after twenty-eight weeks of the pregnancy you keep your right to time off for post-natal visits.

Apprenticeship, probation or training
Your period of apprenticeship, probation or training is put on hold during maternity leave, the balance of the relevant period of time to be completed on your return to work.

Basic maternity leave

Your basic maternity leave entitlement consists of fourteen weeks' paid leave, plus four weeks' unpaid leave, plus additional unpaid leave to cover special circumstances set out below (see Extra maternity leave below).

Change of ownership

Change of ownership or takeover of your company does not in any way lessen the rights or obligations you have under the Act. The new employer has the same responsibilities and obligations as your old employer, as you do.

Dismissal

Dismissal or notice of dismissal including redundancy or suspension or notice of suspension cannot be given or served on a woman on maternity leave. From October 1994 the onus of proof will be on the employer to prove that your dismissal was not linked to your pregnancy (see also Unfair Dismissals Act).

Disputes

Disputes about matters covered by this Act can be dealt with by any of the following:

❑ the Rights Commissioner or the Employment Appeals Tribunal
❑ your trade union, which will advise you of your rights and if necessary represent you at any or all of the above levels.

Extra maternity leave

Extra maternity leave in excess of the basic fourteen weeks' entitlement is allowed where:

❑ the woman decides to take an additional four weeks' unpaid leave. No reason need be given but the employee must notify the employer in writing

❏ the birth is delayed and this has the effect of leaving less than four weeks' leave after the birth, in which case the woman is entitled to take additional leave to ensure four weeks' leave after the birth. You are expected to notify your employer of your need to take additional leave as soon as possible
❏ it is indicated by reason of a health or safety hazard in the workplace.

Health and safety

The European Union Pregnancy Directive, which has effect from October 1994, obliges your employer to identify and advise you of any workplace health or safety risk to your pregnancy. The employer must avoid exposing you to risk, if necessary by reorganising your working conditions, working time, or by your transfer. If these alternatives are not practical you must be given time off work or an extension of maternity leave.

Holiday entitlement

Holiday entitlement continues to be earned during maternity leave (see also Holiday (Employees) Act) and you continue to be entitled to public holidays which occur during your maternity leave.

Miscarriage

Should you have a miscarriage in the first twenty-six weeks of pregnancy you will not be entitled to maternity leave.

Notice

You are obliged to give your employer at least four weeks' written notice of your intention to take maternity leave and provide a medical certificate confirming pregnancy and the expected date of confinement. Notice to the employer of your intention to return to work must be given in writing at least four weeks before the intended date of return.

1st notice	This is best done at the same time as you are giving written notification to the employer of your intention of taking maternity leave.
2nd notice	You must notify your employer again in writing at least two weeks before the expected date of return to work.
	In other words the employer is entitled to *two written notices* from you of your intended date of return. This is important as failure to give these written notifications
Loss of job	may lead to your losing your right to return to work.

Pay increases

Pay increases awarded during maternity leave must be applied to you.

Payment

Payment by the Department of Social Welfare during maternity leave is for fourteen weeks and provides for 70 per cent of the average earnings of the relevant tax year, i.e. the previous tax year. There is a minimum payment per week. To qualify for payment you must have made at least thirty-nine social welfare contributions either:

❏ in the twelve months prior to maternity leave, *or*
❏ in the last 'social welfare contribution year' before the benefit year in which the claim is made, *or*
❏ in a subsequent benefit year.

Make sure you claim the benefit at least four weeks prior to the commencement of the maternity leave, to ensure prompt payment. You can obtain the necessary forms from the Department of Social Welfare in Dublin or any local office.

Post-natal

See Antenatal or Post-natal above.

Premature birth	If premature birth occurs when you are on maternity leave, it does not affect the dates already notified, i.e. the date of return to work remains the same.
Return to work	Your right to return to work is guaranteed as long as you comply with the notification procedures and the specified leave periods set out above.
Sick leave	Where you have an occupational sick pay scheme your paid sick leave entitlement cannot be reduced by reference to your having taken maternity leave.
What job do I return to?	The Act states that you should return to the same job, in the same place, on the same grade, with the same or higher pay. Your contract of employment should be unchanged. However, if your employer cannot for practical reasons give you back your exact job then alternative work can be offered.
When to take maternity leave	The fourteen weeks of maternity leave should normally be taken in the following manner:

❏ four weeks before the expected birth
❏ four weeks after the birth
❏ with the remaining six weeks being taken either before or after the birth, as decided by you.

MINIMUM NOTICE AND TERMS OF EMPLOYMENT ACTS 1973–1991

[This Act should be read in conjunction with the Terms of Employment (Information) Act 1994]

Purpose

To provide a worker with notice of dismissal and a legal right to written information regarding terms and conditions of employment.

Who is covered

You are covered if you have been employed for at least eight hours per week and for at least thirteen weeks with the same employer, unless you are employed in any of the following situations:

- ❑ a member of the Garda Síochána
- ❑ a member of the permanent defence forces
- ❑ a civil servant
- ❑ living in the same private house or farm as your employer and being an immediate relative
- ❑ you are 'signing on Articles' under the Merchant Shipping Act.

If your concern relates specifically to information about your contract of employment, you should consult the Terms of Employment (Information) Act 1994, which applies to all workers.

DETAILS AND DEFINITIONS

Calculation of service

Calculation of service includes periods out of work (up to twenty-six weeks) due to sickness, lay-off, injury, lock-outs, or lack of work as a result of a dispute in another company. The period of a strike against your own firm cannot be included in the calculation of your service. If however you are absent with the permission of the employer this period can be included in the calculation, as can service with the reserve defence forces.

Change of ownership

Change of ownership by takeover does not in any way break your continuity of employment, unless you have accepted a redundancy lump sum from the previous owner.

Content of a contract

The content of an employment contract should include:

❑ date of starting work
❑ termination date, if the contract is for a fixed time
❑ period of notice required to be given by either party before the termination of the contract
❑ hours of work
❑ holiday entitlement
❑ pay including basic pay, overtime, shift, bonus, commission etc. plus the method of calculation
❑ pension scheme
❑ sick pay scheme.

The Unfair Dismissals Act requires that employees be issued with dismissal procedures within twenty-eight days of commencing employment.

It is important to consider the Terms of Employment (Information) Act 1994.

| **Disputes** | Disputes regarding any aspect of your contract of employment can be dealt with either by you directly with your employer, or by your trade union. Any matter relating to notice can be the subject of an investigation by the Employment Appeals Tribunal. |

Misconduct   Misconduct by either you or your employer may allow the aggrieved party to terminate the contract without notice.

Notice of termination   Your employer must give you notice of termination of employment which must conform with the following table:

Service	Notice
❏ Over 13 weeks and up to 2 years	1 week
❏ Over 2 years and up to 5 years	2 weeks
❏ Over 5 years and up to 10 years	4 weeks
❏ Over 10 years and up to 15 years	6 weeks
❏ Over 15 years	8 weeks

Payment in lieu   Your employer can pay you a corresponding number of weeks' wages instead of the notice periods specified above.

Notice to Employer   If you are leaving your employment you must give your employer at least one week's notice unless you have a contract of employment that requires you to give more.

Service   Service is considered 'continuous', i.e. not broken for the purpose of calculating your notice entitlement, *unless*

❏ you leave the job voluntarily. This includes opting for redundancy as a result of short time or a period or periods of lay-off, *or*
❏ you are dismissed.

Strikes	Strikes, lock-outs or lay-off periods are included as continuous service but if you are involved in a strike against your own employer the period of the strike cannot be included in calculating your total service.
Terms of employment	Terms of employment must be in writing if requested by an employee and be presented to the employee within two months of the request being made. New employees must be given their terms of employment in writing within one month of starting work. The Terms of Employment (Information) Act 1994 should be consulted for further information on this matter.

PAYMENT OF WAGES ACT 1991

Purpose	To provide a worker with a right to: ❑ an easily usable form of wage payment where cash is not being paid ❑ protection from unlawful deductions, or payments, from wages ❑ a regular written statement of wages (pay slip).
Who is covered	You are covered whether you are employed in the private, public or voluntary sectors, whether you are an apprentice or whether you are under a contract of service through an employment agency contractor or sub-contractor.

DETAILS AND DEFINITIONS

Authorised officers

These are appointed by the Minister for Enterprise and Employment and have the powers to:

❏ enter premises
❏ copy and take away and inspect documents
❏ request and obtain relevant information from any involved person.

Obstruction

Any person(s) impeding or obstructing an officer in the course of his or her duties will be liable to a fine of up to £1,000.

Disputes

If you feel that an unlawful deduction has been made from your wages or salary this can, on your written request or that of your representative, be investigated by a Rights Commissioner or by the Employment Appeals Tribunal.

This should be done *within six months* of the first deduction or payment by, or to, the employer. However, in exceptional circumstances the six months limit can be extended by the Rights Commissioner to a maximum of a further six months.

The law courts can also be used to recover unlawful deductions. If you select the law courts you rule out the use of the Rights Commissioner or the Employment Appeals Tribunal.

Rights Commissioner

Having carried out the investigation the Rights Commissioner will issue a decision. Either the employee or the employer can appeal the decision but must do so *within six weeks* of its date of issue.

Appeals	An appeal is made to the Employment Appeals Tribunal (see separate Section on the Employment Appeals Tribunal), who can decide to uphold, vary or find against the original Rights Commissioner's decision.
Employment Appeals Tribunal	The decision of the Employment Appeals Tribunal is called a 'determination'. It can be appealed by either the employee or the employer to the law courts on a point of law.
Awards	Compensation by the Rights Commissioner or the Employment Appeals Tribunal in respect of each proven unlawful deduction is limited to either of these options:

❏ the remaining wage (net), having taken out all lawful deductions that would have been paid to the person the week before the first unlawful deduction (or payment to the employer)

For example:

Unlawful payment or deduction	£10
Gross weekly wage	£200
Total lawful deductions	£100
Net remaining wage	£100
Maximum compensation	£100
	per unlawful
	deduction

or

❏ twice the amount of the deduction (or payment to the employer) in a situation where the amount deducted was greater than the remaining wage specified above

For example:

Unlawful payment or deduction	£110
Gross weekly wage	£200
Total lawful deductions	£100
Net remaining wage	£100
Maximum compensation	£220
	per unlawful
	deduction.

Implementation	Decisions of the Rights Commissioner or Employment Appeals Tribunal must be implemented *within six weeks* of their being issued unless the decision specifies otherwise. In the absence of an appeal by either party, a failure to implement a decision can be pursued as though it were a Circuit Court order.
Goods and services	Goods and services may form a part of wages or salary package only with your agreement. If at any time you decide not to avail yourself of such goods and services your employer is then obliged to pay in accordance with one of the acceptable systems of payment set out below.
Inability to pay	The inability of your employer to pay you in the normal manner (owing to strikes or industrial action affecting the financial institutions) can, with your agreement, result in your employer's using any other of the acceptable forms of payment listed. Failure to obtain your agreement means the employer must pay the wages or salary in cash.
Law courts	Using the law courts to recover unlawful deductions rules out the option of using the Rights Commissioner and/or the Employment Appeals Tribunal. Equally,

using the Rights Commissioner option rules out the law courts.

Mistakes

Errors on a pay slip or written statement of wages do not invalidate the slip as long as the error was made in good faith.

No cover

You are *not* covered by this Act in respect of the following:

❑ allowance, gratuity or payment made because of death, redundancy, resignation, retirement, dismissal
❑ benefit in kind
❑ payment of expenses incurred by you as a result of the employment
❑ payment made to you for reason(s) outside the scope of your employment
❑ pension payments.

Non-payment of wages

The failure to pay wages or the payment of less wages than due will be considered as an unlawful deduction and as such can be pursued in the manner set out in the Disputes section above.

Pay slip

A written statement of wages, the provision of which is a legal obligation on the employer. It must specify:

❑ the gross wages, *and*
❑ each deduction made.

Credit transfer

It must be issued with every wage or salary payment, except where payment is being made by credit transfer. In this case it should be given to the employee as soon as possible following the transfer of wages.

Payment systems   Acceptable payment systems are:

❏ cash
❏ bank draft or cheque drawn on a commercial or trustee bank
❏ credit transfer with the account being specified by the employee
❏ orders or warrants issued by An Post, a government minister, local authority, health board etc.
❏ other forms of payment listed in the complete Act.

You are entitled to demand payment in cash only where you were paid in cash immediately prior to the coming into force of this Act in 1991, *or* if you are a manual worker who entered into an agreement (under the 1979 Payment of Wages Act) with your employer to be paid other than by cash and the agreement provided for a return to cash payment.

Receipts   Receipts for every payment from an employee to an employer must be issued immediately and the employer is obliged to ensure that the payment is lawful.

Restrictions on employers   When making deductions from wages for such items or services as breakages, cash shortfall, poor work, cleaning of clothing or equipment, fines arising from disciplinary proceedings etc. employers must comply with the following:

Terms of employment   The deduction must be provided for in the written contract or understood in the verbal contract. The Minimum Notice and Terms of Employment Act 1973 and the Terms of Employment (Information) Act 1994 make written terms of employment obligatory for all employees.

Ability to pay	The amount to be deducted must take into account the ability of the employee to pay and be fair in proportion to the wage.
Written notice	Prior to the commencement of the deduction, you must be given written details of the terms of the contract or the wrongdoing that justifies the deduction. In addition, at least one week's notice must be given to you before deductions can start.
Time limit	Deductions or payments must commence *within six months* of the employer's becoming aware of the offence, damage, wrongdoing etc. or of the commencement of the supply of goods or services as part of wages or salary.
Damage	Where the deduction is in respect of damage or loss it can be for no more than the monetary value of the damage or loss sustained. The employer can also impose a disciplinary fine, provided this is allowed for in the contract.
Goods and services	Where goods or services are being supplied to the employee the employer is not entitled to make a profit on the transaction.
Time limit	If you believe that a deduction or payment is unlawful, and you wish to make a written complaint to a Rights Commissioner it must be done *within six months* of the date of
Escape clause	first deduction or payment to the employer. Only in exceptional circumstances can the Rights Commissioner extend this period.

Valid deductions	These are deductions from wages such as the following:
Work related	❏ deductions required by the contract of employment, e.g. pension scheme or other occupational scheme specifically referred to in the contract of employment ❏ deductions arising from industrial action (including strikes) ❏ deductions (or payments) to recover an overpayment
Third parties	❏ deductions to third parties such as credit union, building society, VHI, trade union subscriptions etc., provided you have given prior written permission
Tax, PRSI, court orders etc.	❏ statutory deductions such as tax, PRSI, attachment of earnings orders, statutory disciplinary procedures or deductions arising from court orders.
Complaints procedure	You may use the complaints procedure of the Act only where your employer: ❏ is not paying the correct amount over to a third party ❏ is not paying it by the appropriate dates ❏ is deducting more than the over payment or the amount necessary or agreed ❏ is deducting more than that specified by the statutory body.
Wages	'Wages' are defined in the Act as being any payment or return for work done including:

❏ basic pay	❏ maternity pay
❏ bonus	❏ overtime
❏ commission	❏ payment in lieu of notice
❏ fee	❏ shift payments
❏ holiday pay	❏ sick leave payment.

PENSIONS ACT 1990

Purpose

To provide enhanced protection to a worker as a member of a pension scheme in respect of funding, trustees, disclosure of information, preservation of benefits for early leavers and equality of treatment between men and women.

The Act also established the Pensions Board which is responsible for ensuring that pension schemes comply with the legislation.

Who is covered

All occupational pension schemes are covered by the Act with the exception of 'designated' public service schemes, e.g. university pension funds. Such designated schemes are, nonetheless, covered by those sections of the Act dealing with the provision of information, the obligations on trustees and equality of treatment between men and women.

DETAILS AND DEFINITIONS

Certification

Certification of a pension scheme means that trustees must demonstrate to the satisfaction of the Pensions Board by way of a financial statement/certificate signed by an actuary that the scheme is financially sound. This must be done at least every three-and-a-half years. If the Pensions Board is not satisfied with this statement/certificate they can demand of the trustees and the actuary that a funding plan for the scheme be presented.

Proof of certification

Proof of certification can be demanded by you as an individual member or by an authorised trade union within the context of the scheme's annual report.

Election of trustees	Member trustees, i.e. trustees directly elected by the members of the pension scheme, are provided for if your scheme is a funded scheme with not less than fifty qualified members, or a directly invested scheme with not less than twelve qualified members.
Qualified members	Qualified members consist of active and pensioner members, i.e. those employed and in membership of the scheme and those retired and receiving benefits from the scheme.
Active members	Those in employment for whom a pension is being funded.
Options	The available options are as follows:

❏ retain the existing trustee arrangements (by taking no action)

❏ elect trustees under the 'standard arrangement'. The employer nominates half of the trustees and the qualified members elect the other half. These trustees then elect a chairperson. If they cannot agree among themselves, the employer selects the chairperson.

❏ approve those selected by the employer. This is titled the 'alternative arrangement'. The employer selects all the trustees. In addition the employer can decide who the chairperson will be, or the method of selection of the chairperson.

❏ approve the selection or retention as appropriate of a sole corporate trustee.

Election/selection process	Should you decide not to retain the existing arrangement then you must request that a vote of the qualified members take place. This is called a preliminary poll. The request

must be made in writing to the current trustees *not the employer*. The purpose of the poll is to determine which of the two remaining options of election/selection will be used. For the current trustees to act on such a request it must be supported by

❏ not less than 15 per cent of the qualified members, *or*
❏ an authorised trade union or unions with not less than 50 per cent of the active members, *or*
❏ the main employer.

Notification to employer	The trustees are obliged on receipt of such a written request to notify the employer within fourteen days, appoint a returning officer without delay and provide a list of the qualified members to the returning officer.
Preliminary poll	The purpose of the preliminary poll is to decide which of the above options will apply.
Refusal or failure	If the employer refuses or fails to allow the election process continue, the trustees, *within sixty days*, must instruct the returning officer to continue with the election regardless of the employer's wishes.
How many trustees	You are entitled to elect at least two trustees or half the total number of trustees when the standard arrangement is being used. Where the alternative arrangement is selected the number of trustees is that specified in the preliminary poll.
Returning officer	The returning officer, who is in charge of all aspects of the voting, is selected by the trustees and is either ❏ the company secretary or the person who

carries out the duties of the company secretary, *or*

❏ any other person whom the trustees believe capable of doing the job.

Nominations	Any person, other than the returning officer, can be nominated for election as a member trustee but must be supported by not less than ten qualified members, or 10 per cent of the qualified membership whichever is the lesser *and* they must also indicate their acceptance of the nomination in a manner acceptable to the returning officer.
The chairperson	The chairperson must be selected by the trustees *within thirty days* of the election or selection result. This selection, which may be one of their own number or an extra person, is carried out by agreement of the trustees or failing that the employer makes the selection.
Period of office	Properly appointed member trustees hold their positions for six years.
Filling of vacancies	Vacancies among the member trustees are filled by the next person in the election process who had received the highest number of votes or failing that by any other person selected by the existing member trustees.
Equality	Equality of treatment regardless of sex is stipulated in the Act and therefore no pension scheme can discriminate on these grounds.
Information	Information must be provided to members, prospective members and people who are benefiting from the pension fund such as

dependants of deceased members. You have a right to such information and it must include such matters as:

❏ details of personal entitlements both during service and on leaving it
❏ trustee reports
❏ reports of any investments and the percentage involved
❏ annual accounts of the scheme
❏ actuarial valuations showing the financial health or otherwise of the scheme.

Investigations

Investigations into the management of a pension scheme or any alleged breach of the Pensions Act may be carried out by the Pension Board on receipt of a formal complaint. Any person found to be in breach of the provisions of this Act can face substantial fines as well as imprisonment.

Leaving work

If you leave work before normal retirement age, you may keep the value of your pension and/or transfer it to your new employment. This means you can leave the pension untouched until you reach normal retirement age (this is called a preserved benefit), convert the benefit into a bond, or transfer the benefit to your new employment.

Minimum funding

Minimum funding of a pension scheme is part of the legal obligations on the fund's trustees. This means it is necessary to ensure at all times that there are sufficient funds in the scheme to meet the specified benefits.

Refund of contributions

A refund of your pension contributions can take place in the following circumstances:

❏ If you left work prior to 31.12.'92 or with

less than five years' service you have the option of
– a deferred pension *or*
– a refund of contributions with interest added, less tax.
❏ If you leave after 1.1.'93 with five or more years' service you will be entitled to the options outlined above in respect of service prior to 31.12.'90. Service after 1.1.'91 will attract a preserved benefit and this will be revalued from time to time in accordance with the Act.

Trust deeds

The trust deeds are the fundamental document of the pension scheme. You can request them from the trustees. In any serious dispute they may very well be the deciding factor in the case.

Trustees

Trustees of pension schemes must act in the best interest of the members, ensuring among other matters that the monies are prudently invested, that the information required under the Act is obtained and transmitted to the members and that the scheme is being run in accordance with the trust deeds.

Vested rights

Vested rights normally refer to an earned right to a benefit on leaving an organisation. In many schemes such benefits are subject to a minimum number of years of service and very often are conditional on the employee's resignation being in no way connected with disciplinary matters such as dismissal for reason of misconduct etc.

Vested rights should not be confused with 'preserved benefits' (see *Glossary*).

PROTECTION OF EMPLOYEES (EMPLOYERS' INSOLVENCY) ACTS 1984–1991

Purpose

To provide an employee, in certain circumstances, with protection from pay-related losses when a company becomes insolvent.

Who is covered

You are covered if you are a fully insured employee or a part-time worker, who works for the same employer for at least eight hours per week and for at least thirteen weeks. Those over sixty-six years of age are covered.

DETAILS AND DEFINITIONS

Awards

Awards under the following Acts which have been finalised and the outcome of which has been accepted by you *and* the employer or employer's representative will be honoured:

❏ Redundancy Payments Acts – where for reasons of insolvency your employer cannot pay all or part of a statutory redundancy payment, the Social Insurance Fund will pay the money, subject to certain conditions.
❏ Unfair Dismissals Acts – provided a final decision has been taken on your case, i.e. the allowed time for making an appeal has run out or the appeal has been withdrawn or the appeal has been decided upon. In addition the outcome of the case must have been decided within the eighteen months prior to

the date of insolvency or subsequent to the date of insolvency.

❏ Anti-Discrimination (Pay) and Employment Equality Acts – provided a final decision has been taken on your case, i.e. the allowed time for making an appeal has run out or the appeal has been withdrawn or the appeal has been decided upon. In addition the outcome of the case must have been decided within the eighteen months prior to the date of insolvency or subsequent to the date of insolvency.

❏ Minimum Notice and Terms of Employment Act

❏ Employment Regulation Orders – where before the date of insolvency a claim against the employer has been properly made to the appropriate enforcement agency of the Department of Enterprise and Employment.

❏ Common law damages (maximum allowed 104 weeks' wages) for *wrongful dismissal*.

Closure

Where a closedown of your employment takes place and there are no funds to pay your entitlements, the Social Insurance Fund will compensate you to a limited degree for any proven loss in respect of pay, awards, unpaid pension fund contributions, sick pay etc.

Date of insolvency

The date of insolvency of a company is the date on which one of the following occurs:

❏ bankruptcy is declared

❏ a petition under Deeds of Arrangement Act 1887 is filed

❏ the employer who is insolvent in terms of the Succession Act 1965, dies

❏ a provisional liquidator is appointed

❏ a resolution for the voluntary winding up of the company is passed
❏ a receiver is appointed
❏ possession is taken by or on behalf of a debenture holder.

Deductions

Deductions from pay such as life assurance, union contributions, VHI, are also protected to the extent of eight weeks' deductions, provided these took place within the eighteen months before the date of insolvency.

Disputes

Disputes about any aspect of your rights under this Act in such matters as wages owed, outstanding holiday or sick pay, pension contributions etc., may be dealt with by you or your trade union taking a case to the Employment Appeals Tribunal.

Exclusions

No payment will be made where you and your employer act together to make an application and where your employer could have afforded to pay all or part of the debt outstanding.

Loss of pay

Loss of pay including salary, wages, holiday pay or sick pay which are outstanding on the date the company becomes insolvent and which took place within the eighteen months prior to the date of insolvency will be compensated for up to a maximum of eight weeks' wages.

Maximum amount considered

All payments are subject to a maximum weekly amount decided from time to time by the Department of Enterprise and Employment. At time of publication this was £300 gross per week.
There are statutory time constraints involved.

Payments	Entitlements under this Act are paid by the Social Insurance Fund.
Pension contributions	The Social Insurance Fund will protect the pension contributions of both you and your employer to the extent of:

❏ contributions deducted from salaries in respect of the twelve months preceding insolvency but not paid into the pension fund, *and, in respect of the employer*

❏ the amount necessary to ensure that the pension fund can meet its obligations, *or* the balance of the employer's contributions unpaid in the twelve months prior to the date or insolvency, *whichever is the least expensive.*

PROTECTION OF EMPLOYMENT ACT 1977

Purpose	To provide earlier notification of, and information on, collective redundancies.
Who is covered	Workers other than state employees in companies with over twenty employees.

DETAILS AND DEFINITIONS

Collective redundancies	Collective redundancies are defined as the following:

❏ five redundancies in a company with twenty to forty-nine workers
❏ ten redundancies in a company with fifty to ninety-nine workers
❏ ten per cent of the workforce in a company with a hundred to 299 workers
❏ thirty redundancies in a company with 300 or more workers.

Consultation

Consultation with the employees' representatives must take place at least thirty days before the date on which the redundancies will occur. The purpose of this consultation will be to specify:

❏ the reasons for the redundancies
❏ the basis for selection
❏ the number and category of employees affected
❏ the time scale envisaged for the redundancies to take place
❏ the number of employees in the company.
The consultation will also allow for discussions to avoid or reduce the number of proposed redundancies.

Employee representatives

Employee representatives are defined as officials (including shop stewards) of a trade union or staff association.

Notice

Notice to the Minister for Enterprise and Employment, which should include all the information mentioned above, must be given at least thirty days prior to the proposed date for the collective redundancy.

Notification

Notification or consultation does not affect the rights you have under various pieces of legislation, e.g. minimum notice, redundancy payments, unfair dismissal.

| **Ministerial intervention** | The Minister for Enterprise and Employment *or* an officer acting on behalf of the minister may consult with the employer for the purpose of attempting to seek solutions to the problems caused by the proposed redundancies. The employer must supply the minister with any relevant information required. |

PROTECTION OF YOUNG PERSONS (EMPLOYMENT) ACT 1977

| **Purpose** | To provide young persons with protection on such matters as rest breaks, maximum hours, minimum age, employment records, night work and overtime. |

| **Who is covered** | All workers in paid employment *under* the age of eighteen years. |

DETAILS AND DEFINITIONS

| **Proof of age** | Proof of age must be established by the employer when hiring young people, i.e. those under the age of eighteen years. You may be asked to produce a birth certificate. Where it is intended to employ a child between age fourteen and fifteen the written permission of parent or guardian must be obtained by the employer. |

Breaks from work	A 'young person' must be given a break from work, of at least thirty minutes' duration, for any period of five hours worked. A 'child' must be given a break from work, of at least thirty minutes' duration, for any period of four hours worked. Where more than five days in a week and more than three hours on a Sunday is worked, there is an entitlement to twenty-four hours free from work.
Child	A 'child' is defined as a person under fifteen years of age (the current school leaving age).
Disputes	Disputes in relation to any aspect of this Act may be pursued through the Employment Rights Section of the Department of Enterprise and Employment. The employee, parent or guardian and/or a trade union is entitled to take cases under the legislation.
Fines	Fines of up to £200 plus £20 per day can be imposed on people found to be in breach of this law.
Maximum hours of work	Maximum hours of work allowed are as follows:
fourteen to fifteen years of age (during school term)	❏ A 'child' may not work more than two hours in any weekday and no more than fourteen hours in any week. ❏ All working hours must be outside school time. ❏ Working hours on a Saturday and Sunday may not exceed two hours in total. For example two hours' work on a Saturday prohibits the child working at all on the Sunday.
(outside school term)	❏ fourteen consecutive days clear of work must be taken by a child during the school summer holidays.

❏ A child may work no more than seven hours in any day and no more than thirty-five in any week.

NB A European Union directive will take effect during 1994 making it illegal for any child under fifteen years to work.

fifteen to
sixteen years

A young person between fifteen and sixteen years may work no more than forty hours in any week, of which no more than eight hours are allowed in any day, with the normal working week being 37.5 hours.

sixteen to
eighteen years

A young person between sixteen and eighteen years may work:

❏ no more than 2,000 hours in any year
❏ no more than 172 hours in any four weeks
❏ no more than forty-five hours in any week
❏ no more than nine hours in any day.

The normal working hours are eight in any day, forty in any week.

NB Since this Act was passed the normal working week, in practice, is now thirty-nine hours.

Night work

Night work is restricted in the following manner:
❏ Children under fifteen years of age are not allowed work for a period of fourteen consecutive hours including the hours between 8 pm and 8 am.
❏ Between the ages of fifteen to eighteen a young person may not work for twelve consecutive hours including the hours between 10 pm and 6 am.

Overtime

Overtime is paid at a rate of at least time and a quarter. This is a legal entitlement for all hours worked in excess of normal hours. Any worker under eighteen years of age must be given a thirty-minute break before starting overtime where the overtime period is intended or is likely to exceed 1.5 hours.

Parent

It is an offence for a parent, guardian or employer to allow a child work in excess of that specified in the Act.

Records

Records of the hours of work and ages of employees covered by this Act must be maintained by the employer and be available for inspection.

Reduction of wages

A reduction of wages is illegal where the employer reduces the hours of work in order to comply with this Act.

Various employers

You cannot work more than the total number of allowed hours even where you are employed by various employers.

Young person

A 'young person' is defined as being over fifteen but under eighteen years of age.

REDUNDANCY PAYMENTS ACTS 1967–1991

Purpose

To provide a worker with a lump sum payment, subject to certain conditions, on loss of a job by reason of redundancy.

Who is covered

You are covered if you are between the ages of sixteen and sixty-six, and have been employed for 104 or more weeks with the same employer and for eight hours or more per week.

DETAILS AND DEFINITIONS

Acceptance of redundancy

Acceptance of a redundancy payment means that you break your service. If you are re-employed by the same employer at a later date you will be considered in all respects a new employee.

Alternative work

Where your employer offers you alternative work you may not be entitled to redundancy payments if:

❏ you accept or unreasonably refuse to accept immediate re-employment on terms that do not differ from your previous written or verbal contract *or*

❏ you accept or unreasonably refuse to accept suitable re-employment, within four weeks of your having been made redundant, on terms which differ from your previous written or verbal contract *or*

❏ you accept alternative work on a trial basis of more than four weeks' duration *or*

❏ you accept, on a temporary basis, a

reduction in pay and/or hours of work, of not less than half of your previous contract and for more than a period of fifty-two weeks.

Apprentices

If during the period of your apprenticeship you are made redundant you are entitled to redundancy payments provided you meet the legal requirements for those covered above.

If, however, you are made redundant within one month of the end of your apprenticeship, you will not be entitled to redundancy payment.

Claiming redundancy

Your employer is obliged to provide you with a certificate of redundancy. This must specify that your dismissal is due to redundancy. The signed document, with the original signatures, must be forwarded to the Department of Enterprise and Employment. Failure to comply with this requirement will leave your employer open to fines of £300 per offence and loss of the 60 per cent rebate of any statutory redundancy payments made.

Calculating redundancy payment

To be covered by the Act you need at least 104 weeks' employment with the same employer. It is important to note that the 104 weeks need not necessarily be 104 weeks actually worked, for example:

❏ if your employer dismissed you without giving you due notice (see the Minimum Notice and Terms of Employment Act) and this period of notice, if added to your service, would have given you the 104 weeks required, then you are covered by the Act.
❏ absence due to lay off or sickness does not break your service in terms of acquiring the 104 weeks required.

You will need to be familiar with formulas and terms to calculate your redundancy payment. These are set out below. (See 'continuous service', 'reckonable service' and 'calculating reckonable service'.)

Continuous service

No period of employment outside a period of continuous employment can be included in the calculation of your redundancy payment.

Service may be considered 'continuous' provided it is not broken by

❏ your voluntary resignation from the company
❏ you dismissal, unless
– it is reversed by the Employment Appeals Tribunal as an unfair dismissal *or*
– in the case of a redundancy you are dismissed before reaching the qualifying period of 104 weeks and are re-employed within twenty-six weeks of the dismissal
– you are re-employed by an associated company within four weeks of the dismissal
❏ your death
❏ lay-off in excess of twenty-six consecutive weeks
❏ holidays in excess of twenty-six consecutive weeks
❏ sickness or injury in excess of seventy-eight consecutive weeks
❏ authorised absence in excess of twenty-six consecutive weeks
❏ maternity leave in excess of that provided by the Maternity (Protection of Employees) Act 1981.

Continuous service is not broken by any period of absence in respect of strikes, lock-outs or service in the reserve defence forces.

Disputes	In any dispute regarding whether or not your service was continuous, the Employment Appeals Tribunal will assume it was continuous unless the employer can prove the opposite.

Reckonable service	When calculating your lump sum you are entitled to include all your 'reckonable service' (see *Glossary*). In this calculation you can include absence from work by reason of sickness, holidays, maternity leave, or absence with the permission of the employer etc., subject to the limitations set out below:

❏ occupational injury/disease – up to fifty-two weeks
❏ other injury or disease – up to twenty-six weeks
❏ maternity leave – up to fourteen weeks
❏ strikes – any amount of weeks may be included if they occurred before 1968; periods on strike after 1968 may not be included in the calculation
❏ lock out – any number of weeks may be included
❏ absence authorised by the employer – up to thirteen weeks in any fifty-two may be included
❏ service abroad – any number of weeks may be included.

No period of lay-off can be included in the calculation of reckonable service.

Calculating reckonable service	Your service is calculated as follows:

❏ each full year counts as 364 days *plus*
❏ each part of a year specified in surplus days, *plus*

❏ a day for each year of service, *plus*
❏ a day for each leap year.

For example, say your 'reckonable service' is ten years, five months and three weeks

Full years (10 x 364)		= 3,640 days
Surplus days		
Part Year = 5 months (Jan-May)=		151 days
plus 3 weeks	=	21 days
A day for each year of service	=	10 days
A day for each leap year	=	2 days
	Total	184 days

Total reckonable service is therefore ten years and 184 days. This will give eleven years reckonable service, because surplus days in excess of 182 days (twenty-six weeks) entitle you to an additional full year's 'reckonable service'.

Doubts on accuracy

If you have any doubt about the accuracy of your employer's calculation you should consult the Redundancy Payments Section of the Department of Enterprise and Employment or the Employment Appeals Tribunal, or your trade union who will advise you.

The amount

The amount of money (lump sum) to which you may be entitled is calculated on the following basis:

❏ a half week's pay for each year of service prior to age forty-one and
❏ one week's pay for each year of service over forty-one
❏ plus one week's pay.

| Employer's rebate | The employer is entitled to obtain up to 60 per cent rebate of the statutory moneys paid to redundant employees. |

| Larger lump sums | Larger lump sums than provided for under the Act can be paid and often arise from trade union negotiations, sometimes involving the Labour Relations Commission and the Labour Court, or where the company involved is financially capable. The employer is entitled to claim a rebate of 60 per cent only of the statutory redundancy payments made. |

Change of ownership

Where a change of ownership occurs you will not be entitled to redundancy payments in the following circumstances:

❏ where the new owner continues your employment without a break. This means your service is unbroken should a redundancy take place at any later date, *or*

❏ where you accept, or unreasonably refuse, an offer of work from the new employer on the same terms and conditions of employment as your previous written or verbal contract, provided this offer is made within four weeks of your having been made redundant, *or*

❏ where the change of ownership refers only to the property where your place of employment was located, *or*

❏ where an agency, franchise or tenancy is transferred and you accept, or unreasonably refuse, an offer of employment on the same or not substantially different terms as your previous written or verbal contract. This offer must be made within four weeks of the transfer having taken place.

Death	If you die after notice of redundancy has been issued, this does not alter the obligation on the employer to pay the lump sum to your estate.
Offer of renewal or re-engagement	If you die without having decided on an offer of renewal of contract or re-engagement and the offer had not been withdrawn *no* redundancy payment is due.
Lay-off or short-time	If you die within seven days of having given notice of your intention to claim redundancy on the basis of lay-off or short-time *no* redundancy payment is due.
Definition of redundancy	A redundancy is where your employer needs to re-organise the company, the consequences of which are any of the following:

❏ partial or complete closedown
❏ a requirement for fewer employees
❏ a requirement for employees with different skills or knowledge or qualifications.

Voluntary redundancy	If a genuine redundancy occurs and your employer gives the option of allowing you to volunteer for redundancy this does not affect your right to a redundancy payment.
Disputes	The Employment Appeals Tribunal investigates any dispute you might have with regard to your rights under the Redundancy Payment Acts.
Time limit	Your claim can only be heard if, within fifty-two weeks of being made redundant, you have sought, in writing, a lump sum payment from your employer or you have written to the tribunal making a claim.

Exception	Where the tribunal is satisfied that there were reasonable grounds for your not having made a claim within the fifty-two weeks, it has the discretion to extend the period to a maximum of 104 weeks from the date of the dismissal.
Employer's death	If your employer dies, the following circumstances apply:
Offer of renewal or re-engagement	If the deceased employer's representative offers you renewal or re-engagement within eight weeks of the death of the employer you will not be considered to have been dismissed which means your service is unbroken.
Refusal of offer	If your refuse a reasonable offer of a job on the same terms with or without a break in employment, or on different but suitable terms, with or without a break of employment not exceeding eight weeks, you will not be entitled to redundancy payment.
Lay-off or short-time	If you had served notice on your employer of your intention to seek redundancy and the employer died within four weeks of this notice, you will be entitled to a redundancy payment, provided the deceased employer's representative keeps you on lay-off or short-time or does not re-engage you during the four weeks after you gave in your notice.
Failure to notify	Failure by the employer to carry out the proper notification procedures to employees and the Department of Enterprise and Employment, may result in the loss to the employer of a rebate which can amount to 60 per cent of the total paid out under the Act.
Failure to pay	Where your employer fails to pay part or all of your entitlement, the Social Insurance

Fund will pay the amount due on receipt of either the redundancy certificate (see Claiming redundancy) or a decision of the Employment Appeals Tribunal. However

❏ you must have taken all reasonable steps to obtain payment including a written request for payment to your employer *or*
❏ your employer must be insolvent *or*
❏ your employer must have died and payment to you would therefore be delayed until the employer's financial affairs were settled.

Leaving before expiry of notice

Your entitlement to redundancy payment is not affected where your employer agrees to your leaving employment prior to the expiry of your redundancy notice. However, if your employer makes a written request that you do not leave until the expiry of notice, or on a date later than you propose, and you unreasonably refuse to comply with this request, you may then lose your right to a redundancy payment.

Maternity leave

If you are on maternity leave when a redundancy situation occurs, the effective date of redundancy cannot be any earlier than the date you had specified as your date of return to work following maternity leave.

Maximum

The maximum amount of weekly pay taken into consideration in calculating redundancy payment is currently £300 per week. This figure is revised from time to time by the Department of Enterprise and Employment.

Notice of redundancy

Notice of redundancy or payment in lieu must be granted in accordance with your length of service with the company. (See

Minimum Notice and Terms of Employment Act).

Notifying the Minister	In accordance with the Protection of Employment Act, the employer is obliged to notify the Minister for Enterprise and Employment of any proposed collective redundancy.
Notice on maternity leave	The effective date of any redundancy notice to you if you are on maternity leave can be no earlier than that specified by you as your date of return to work.

Rehired

If you are rehired by the same employer within twenty-six weeks, and where no redundancy compensation was paid, your service is unbroken.

By a subsidiary

Rehire by an associated or subsidiary company within four weeks of a dismissal also means your service is unbroken and continuous.

Short time or lay-off

Short time working and/or lay-off will allow you to claim redundancy payment in the following circumstances:

❏ if your are laid off or on short time for four consecutive weeks *or*
❏ if you are laid off or on short time for any six weeks in thirteen.

If the employer has work for you within four weeks of short-time or lay-off, and states that the work will last for at least thirteen weeks, this would cancel your redundancy claim.

Strikes or lock-outs

Periods where you were involved in either a lock-out or a strike *cannot* be included in the above calculations.

Taxation/Social Welfare	Taxation laws and social welfare regulations allow that redundancy lump sums are tax free up to £6,000, with a further £4,000 tax free added where no previous redundancy payment was made and where there are no other tax free payments being made. An amount of £500 tax free per year of service is allowed.
Withholding social welfare	If your total redundancy package is worth in excess of £15,000 you may be debarred from social welfare benefit for up to nine weeks.
Time off to seek work	You are entitled to reasonable paid time off in the two weeks prior to the proposed date of your redundancy to seek alternative employment. Your employer may request you to provide proof regarding attendance at interviews etc., which you are obliged to provide on condition that it does not damage your chances of obtaining employment.
Transfer	Where you transfer to another company, both employers can agree that your service is continuous. In this situation your total service, in both companies, can be included in the calculation of your redundancy payment if at some later stage the second company makes you redundant. It is advisable to obtain such an agreement between the two employers in writing.
Unfair selection	Selection for redundancy must be fair and must respect any existing agreement on selection, if such an agreement exists in your workplace. For example, if you are selected for redundancy and there are employees with less service and these employees have the same or less required skills than you, then this may constitute an unfair dismissal on grounds of unfair selection for redundancy.

Week's pay	A week's pay includes all earnings. If you are in receipt of accommodation, food, board, lodging or any other benefit in kind etc., an amount to the value of the benefit should be included in the calculation of the week's pay.
Piece or shift workers	In order to decide the weekly pay of a piece or shift worker the following formula applies:

❏ Your *total pay earned* in the twenty-six weeks prior to the thirteen weeks before the expiry date of your redundancy notice, *divided* by the total number of hours worked in the same period, *multiplied* by the normal weekly hours worked on the date you were declared redundant.

No normal hours	The formula used to calculate weekly pay in this case is as follows:

❏ the *total earnings* (including basic, bonus, allowance, commission etc.) in the fifty-two weeks prior to the expiry date of the redundancy notice *divided* by fifty-two.

Overtime	Where you are normally expected to work overtime, your average weekly pay is arrived at by including in the calculation the *total overtime earnings* in the twenty-six weeks prior to the thirteen weeks before the expiry date of your redundancy notice, *divided* by twenty-six.
Working abroad	Provided you were domiciled in Ireland before being sent abroad and were in Ireland on the date of the redundancy, unless your employer did not give you a reasonable opportunity of coming home, you *are* entitled to a redundancy payment.

| Foreign redundancy | Any redundancy payment to which you are entitled under the law of a foreign state will be deducted from your Irish redundancy entitlement. |

SAFETY, HEALTH AND WELFARE AT WORK ACT 1989

| **Purpose** | To extend legislative cover and to establish a National Authority for Occupational Safety and Health. |

| **Who is covered** | Everybody in paid employment including the employer, the self-employed, the employees, the designers and manufacturers of systems, equipment or furniture, as well as members of the public. |

DETAILS AND DEFINITIONS

| **Consultation** | Consultation with the workforce on questions of safety and health is an obligation on the employer. This includes consulting the workforce on the design of systems, type and operation of machinery or equipment, and the handling of materials. |

| **Designers, suppliers, manufacturers** | Designers, suppliers and manufacturers are responsible for making sure that their product, if used properly in accordance with the instructions and design limitations, will not cause any injury to the user. |

Duties of employees

Employees are obliged:

❑ to avoid causing injury to themselves or others
❑ to report dangers in the workplace to the employer
❑ to make use of any article provided for health or safety reasons.

National Safety Authority

The National Safety Authority is responsible for providing guidance and advice on all matters associated with safety and health. Other powers, duties and responsibilities include:

❑ development and establishment of 'codes of practice' and regulations for various aspects of safety and health at work
❑ bringing employers to court for failure to comply with the Act
❑ issuing legally enforceable instructions to make safe a system, operation, material, machine or equipment
❑ obliging an employer to cease operating (either in part or in whole) in the event of any threat to health and safety
❑ enforcement of the Act through a body of inspectors.

Powers of safety representatives

Safety representative(s) who are elected from among the workforce have the following powers:

❑ the right to represent the workforce in consultation and discussion with the employer and/or the inspector from the National Authority for Occupational Safety and Health

❏ the right to paid leave or time off to attend appropriate training/education courses
❏ the right to investigate accidents, hazards or dangers at work.

Protection

Protection of the health and safety of a workforce or any other person who happens to be on the premises is a prime responsibility of the employer. In other words the employer must ensure that the equipment, systems of production, materials, the work area itself and its environs are safe.

Safety statements

Safety statements must be prepared by the employer in consultation with the employees. These statements must include:

❏ the regulations for the safe operation of systems, equipment, machinery and materials
❏ the identification of workplace hazards, dangers and risks
❏ the publication of the names of the people with responsibility for safety and health in your workplace.

Self-employed

Self-employed people are responsible under this Act for ensuring that they do not put either themselves or others in danger through their use or installation of equipment, machinery, materials or systems.

SAFETY IN INDUSTRY ACT 1980

Purpose

To provide for the establishment of safety committees, delegates and representatives and to modernise the Factories Act 1955.

Who is covered

All workers previously covered by the Factories Act 1955.

DETAILS AND DEFINITIONS

Employer

The employer, or nominee, is obliged to attend the first safety committee meeting and has the right to attend all subsequent safety committee meetings. The employer must also give due regard to the representations made by the safety committee or representative.

Experience

The Act advises that if you wish to seek election as safety delegate you should have about two years' experience in the type of work that you will be required to represent.

Failure to elect

Failure of the workers to take the initiative and elect the safety committee or representative within a period of six months means that the employer, within three months, will select the safety committee or representative having first consulted the workforce. Such appointees will hold office for three years.

Functions and responsibilities

Functions and responsibilities of safety committees include the following:

❏ making representations on behalf of the

workforce to the employer who must give
due regard to these views

❑ consulting with and being consulted by the
employer with regard to appropriate safety
and health questions

❑ requesting an investigation by the
inspector under the Act and considering the
inspector's report

❑ ensuring the workforce comply with safety
systems and regulations.

Inspector

The presence of an inspector on the premises
must be reported by the employer to the
safety committee, safety delegate or safety
representative.

Meetings

Meetings of the safety committee may take
place within working hours with no loss of
pay provided they:

❑ are not held more than once every two
months (excluding emergency meetings)

❑ last no more than two hours

❑ do not cause major problems for
production

❑ have a quorum of not less than three
members.

The duration, frequency, standing orders,
quorum etc. are a matter for the committee to
decide.

Names

Names of the members of the safety
committee, delegates or representatives must
be placed by the employer in the general
register of the company. Any changes must
be recorded.

**Safety
committees**

Safety committees may be established in
factories with more than twenty workers.
These committees are made up of worker

and company representatives on the following basis:

Committee Membership

Employee nos.	Worker reps.	Company reps.	Total reps.
❏ 21 to 60	2	1	3
❏ 61 to 80	3	1	4
❏ 81 to 100	3	2	5
❏ 101 to 120	4	2	6
❏ 121 to 140	5	2	7
❏ 141 to 160	6	2	8
❏ 161 to 180	6	3	9
❏ 181 and over	7	3	10

Safety delegate

A safety delegate can be selected by the safety committee but only from among the worker representatives. The duties and powers of the safety delegate include:

❏ acting on behalf of the safety committee in respect of consultation and representation to the employer or an inspector or the workforce
❏ attending with an inspector on a regular inspection round.

Safety representative

The safety representative is elected for a three-year period where the workforce number less than twenty. The functions, duties and responsibilities are similar to those of the safety committee.

Safety statement

The safety statement which must be prepared by the employer in consultation with the workers should include the risks, safety regulations and systems operating within the company and must be presented to the safety committee for their consideration and comment.

TERMS OF EMPLOYMENT (INFORMATION) ACT 1994

Purpose

To provide employees with a right to written information regarding their employment contract or relationship.

Who is covered

You are covered where you have been employed for at least a month and are normally expected to work at least eight hours per week whether employed in the public, private or voluntary sector, as an apprentice or under a contract of service through an employment agency, contractor or sub-contractor.

DETAILS AND DEFINITIONS

Appeals

Where either you or your employer are dissatisfied with a recommendation of a Rights Commissioner it must be appealed to the Employment Appeals Tribunal for a determination within six weeks of its having been issued.

Failure to implement a recommendation	Where your employer has failed to implement a Rights Commissioner's recommendation, and the six weeks' time limit for lodging an appeal has lapsed, you can request the Employment Appeals Tribunal to issue a determination; it must conform with the Rights Commissioner's recommendation. The tribunal must issue this determination without hearing the employer or new evidence.
Failure to implement a determination	Should your employer fail to implement a determination of the Employment Appeals Tribunal within six weeks of its date of issue you, your trade union or the Minister for Enterprise and Employment can request the District Court to issue an order. This order must comply with the details of the determination of the Employment Appeals Tribunal and be issued without hearing the employer or new evidence.
High Court	Either you or your employer can appeal a determination of the Employment Appeals Tribunal to the High Court on a point of law.
Change of contract	If your contract of employment was issued after the coming into force of this Act, then any change to it must be notified to you in writing within one month of the change having taken place *or*, where you will be working abroad, it must be notified to you prior to your departure.
New contracts	
Old contracts	Changes to contracts issued before the coming into force of this Act need *not* be notified to you (except under the Unfair Dismissals Acts in respect of disciplinary procedures), *unless* you have requested your employer to comply with this Act by issuing

you with a written contract which specifies the matters set out in Content of contract below. Your employer has two months to comply with your request and failure to do so can be referred initially to a Rights Commissioner.

Change of ownership

Where you have or are processing a complaint and a change of ownership occurs, the new employer is responsible for settling the matter in dispute or complying with a recommendation, determination or order issued.

Collective agreements, regulations etc.

Your employer is allowed to make reference, without elaboration, to agreements, regulations, statutes etc., where these are either reasonably available for reading during employment *or* reasonably accessible in some other way.

Compensation or redress

Having investigated your complaint the Rights Commissioner may:

❑ decide that the complaint was not well founded so you lose your claim *or*
❑ confirm the accuracy of the contract *or*
❑ alter or add to the contract for the purpose of correcting any inaccuracy or omission. Such an alteration or addition will be considered to have been made by the employer *or*
❑ ask that the employer provide you with a written statement covering any matter specified by the Commissioner *or*
❑ decide that payment of up to four weeks' pay be made in compensation

Interest

If you have been obliged to take your claim to the District Court, it can order payment of interest on any compensation due.

Content of contract

Your contract of employment must be *in writing, signed and dated* and be provided to you within two months of your commencing work *or*, if you were employed before this Act came into force, within two months of your making a request for such a contract. It must include the following matters:

❏ the name of both you and your employer
❏ the address or registered office of the company
❏ the place of work or if no permanent place exists a statement to that effect
❏ the job title or a description of the nature of the work
❏ the date of commencement of employment
❏ in respect of temporary, fixed term or purpose contracts the expected duration and date of termination of the contract
❏ the rate of pay, method of calculation and frequency of payment, e.g. weekly, fortnightly, monthly, etc.
❏ hours of work including overtime
❏ entitlement to paid leave
❏ occupational schemes such as pension, sick pay, etc
❏ the period of notice required
❏ a reference to any collective agreement affecting the terms of the contract whether or not the employer is a party to the agreement
❏ information regarding the institutions or organisations which drew up a collective agreement, regulation etc., which affects the terms of the contract.

If you are working abroad you are entitled to all of the above plus other matters set out in Working abroad below.

Disputes   If you have a dispute regarding any aspect of this Act you should refer it to a Rights Commissioner. The recommendation of the Rights Commissioner can, within six weeks of its being issued, be appealed to the Employment Appeals Tribunal. The investigation by the Rights Commissioner takes place *in private*.

Employment Appeals Tribunal   You should refer to the particular section in this book on how the Employment Appeals Tribunal functions.

Fines   If you or your employer fail or refuse to attend at the Employment Appeals Tribunal, give evidence or produce documents you can be fined up to £1,000 per offence.

Leaving work   Leaving work affects your rights under this Act in two ways:

❏ the Act does not apply if you have been in the continuous service of the employer for less than one month
❏ if you wish to make a complaint under this Act you must do so within six months of having left the employment otherwise you lose your right to so do.

No cover   No cover is provided by this Act to contracts or employment relationships entered into prior to May 1994, *unless* an employee requests that a contract be issued under this Act.

Powers of the Minister   The Minister for Enterprise and Employment has power to alter the required contents of a contract of employment by either adding, deleting or varying the requirements set out in 'Content of contract' above.

| **Records** | Your employer is obliged to maintain a copy of your contract of employment for the period of your employment *plus* one year. |

Requesting a contract

If you became an employee after the coming into force of this Act in May 1994 you have an automatic right to a written contract, and to use the complaints procedure of this Act. If however you were an employee before May 1994, you must request your employer to issue you with a contract under this Act if you wish to enjoy its protections and procedures. Your employer is obliged to comply with your request within two months.

Rights Commissioner

For more detailed information on the role, functions and operating procedures of the Rights Commissioner you should consult the Industrial Relations Act on page 54.

Time limits

The time limits specified in this Act are:

❏ to make a claim having left employment – within six months of resignation
❏ to issue a contract to a new employee – within two months
❏ to issue a contract to a current employee who has made such a request – within two months
❏ to notify a change in a contract – within one month
❏ to notify a change in a contract where the employee will be working abroad for more than one month – date of departure at the latest.

Working abroad

If you are obliged to work abroad for more than one month your employer is obliged to provide you with a written contract *prior to your departure* containing, in addition to those matters specified in Content of contract above, the following:

❏ the period of employment outside the state
❏ the currency in which you will be paid
❏ any other benefits in cash or kind that will be provided
❏ the terms and conditions which will apply to your return home.

UNFAIR DISMISSALS ACTS 1977–1993

Purpose

To protect an employee against unfair or unreasonable dismissal.

Who is covered

You are covered if you have been employed by the same employer for more than 365 days *unless:*

Not covered

❏ you are over sixty-six or under sixteen years of age
❏ you are employed in the officer grade of local authorities, committees of agriculture, civil service, or temporary officer grade of health boards
❏ you are on probation and there is a written contract which sets out the period of probation to be one year or less (except if the dismissal is wholly or mainly owing to trade union activity or pregnancy)

□ you are a student nurse or other paramedic student (except if the dismissal is wholly or mainly owing to trade union activity or pregnancy)

□ you are a member of the defence forces or the Gardaí

□ you are working for and living with a close relative in the same house or farm

□ your dismissal consists only of the specified date of termination of a fixed term or fixed purpose contract

□ you are a FÁS designated apprentice and are dismissed during the first six months of apprenticeship, or within a month of its termination.

DETAILS AND DEFINITIONS

Appeals

If you or your employer are dissatisfied with a Rights Commissioner's recommendation and you wish to appeal it to the Employment Appeals Tribunal, you must do so *within six weeks* of its being issued. Where your employer neither implements nor appeals a decision on unfair dismissal, you can appeal to the Employment Appeals Tribunal for implementation.

Employment Appeals Tribunal

When seeking the implementation of a determination of the Employment Appeals Tribunal an application must be made to the Circuit Court *within six weeks* from the date on which the tribunal communicates its finding to the parties. The court may order your employer to pay you compensation where a determination of the Employment Appeals Tribunal was neither appealed nor implemented, or where an order of the circuit court was not carried out. The court also has the right to change a determination from reinstatement/re-engagement to financial compensation.

Calculation of service

Calculation of service can include twenty-six weeks' absence caused by lay-off, lock-outs, sickness, injury or leave taken with the permission of the employer. Any period when you are on strike against your employer cannot be included in the calculation of total service.

Change of ownership

Where you have been dismissed and are processing a case for unfair dismissal and a change of ownership occurs, the new owner becomes responsible for your dismissal.

Compensation

Compensation to you for the loss of a job through unfair dismissal is determined by a Rights Commissioner initially or on appeal, or directly by the Employment Appeals Tribunal. Compensation can take the form of any of the following:

❑ money – up to two years' loss of salary, or where no financial loss has occurred, up to four weeks' pay. Any payment you receive from social welfare or income tax will be ignored when calculating your financial loss.
❑ re-instatement – this means re-employment in your post, to take effect from the date of the dismissal
❑ re-engagement – this means re-employment in a new or the old post, from a date later than the date of dismissal.

The tribunal is obliged to explain why it chose a particular form of compensation.

Constructive dismissal

The creation by an employer of conditions so intolerable and unreasonable that an employee feels compelled to resign from the employment

Continuous service

Continuous service can be broken only where:

❏ you are dismissed and not immediately re-hired or re-instated by the Employment Appeals Tribunal
❏ you voluntarily leave the job

Fixed term or fixed purpose contracts

❏ there is a series of fixed term or fixed purpose contracts with more than three months' 'break of service' between any two consecutive contracts.

Contract work

If you are employed on a fixed term or fixed purpose contract and are dismissed, you may have grounds for an unfair dismissal claim in the following circumstances:

Union activity or pregnancy

❏ where you are dismissed mainly or wholly because of your pregnancy or trade union activity

Make-up of contract

❏ where there is no written contract or where the contract is not signed or where the contract fails to state that the Unfair Dismissals Act does not apply

❏ where a Rights Commissioner or Employment Appeals Tribunal believes your contract was designed to deprive you of protection under the Act

Re-hired

❏ where you are dismissed and then re-hired within three months to the same or similar post and subsequently dismissed

Replaced	❑ where you are dismissed but the post continues to exist and is filled by another person
Equality	❑ where you are dismissed solely or mainly because of your involvement in processing an equal pay or employment equality claim.
Death	The death of the person seeking redress for unfair dismissal need not affect the claim as a representative of the deceased can continue to process the claim.
Disciplinary procedures	Procedures covering dismissal and/or suspension must be in writing and made available to you *within twenty-eight days* of your starting work. If these are changed you must be advised of this fact *within twenty-eight days*.
Discrimination	Race, colour, creed, sexual orientation, age, being a member of the travelling community or holding certain political beliefs are not grounds for a fair dismissal.
Disputes about dismissal	Disputes about your dismissal can be dealt with by you personally, by your union or by a solicitor. The normal method of having an unfair dismissal case processed is by referring it to either a Rights Commissioner or direct to the Employment Appeals Tribunal. If your employer wishes to object to a hearing by a Rights Commissioner, this objection must be made within twenty-one days of your employer having been notified or else the hearing must go ahead. Normally you must make your claim within six months of the dismissal's having taken place. The time limit can in exceptional circumstances be extended to twelve months (see Time limit below).

Employment agencies	If you are dismissed by a contracted employer (the employer to whom you have been contracted), and this dismissal is found to be unfair in the terms of the Unfair Dismissals Amendment Act 1993, this employer rather than the agency will be liable regardless of who is paying the wages or the existence or not of a contract between the agency and the contracted employer.
Fair dismissal	Grounds for a fair dismissal include questions about your ability to carry out the job, your conduct, redundancy, or if your continued employment would break the law.
Foreign employment	You are covered by the Act where:

❑ you were resident in this state for the duration of the contract, *or*
❑ you were domiciled in this state for the duration of the contract and the employer was resident in this state or the company had its main office or principal place of business in this state.

Illegal contracts	If your contract of employment, written or verbal, had the effect of causing non-payment of income tax or social insurance contributions due, this will not affect your right to protection from unfair dismissal. However, in such circumstances, the appropriate authority will be notified of any outstanding debts to Social Welfare or to the Revenue Commissioners.
Proving the case	The onus of proof lies with the employer. This means that the Employment Appeals Tribunal or the Rights Commissioner must assume the sacking was unfair unless the employer has shown otherwise. In other

words the burden of proving the case is on the employer, not the employee.

There are two exceptions to this rule, i.e. dismissal due to trade union activity, and constructive dismissal.

Immediate dismissal   Immediate dismissal is allowable for gross misconduct, e.g. assault, robbery, fraud etc. However, instant dismissal does not affect your rights under the Act.

Labour Court   The Labour Court represents an option of dealing with your dismissal as does the Labour Relations Commission. However, neither of these can be used if a Rights Commissioner's recommendation has been issued under the Unfair Dismissals Act or if the Employment Appeals Tribunal has started to hear your case.

Law courts   Law courts continue to be an option for the worker seeking compensation for wrongful dismissal. However, you must make a decision to go through the law courts or through the Rights Commissioner and/or the Employment Appeals Tribunal. Deciding on one option automatically excludes the possibility of using the other.

Lock-outs   These are a form of dismissal and are not considered unfair where the worker is re-employed at the end of the lock-out period.

Obstruction of the tribunal   A failure to attend, refusal to give evidence or failure or refusal to provide requested documents to an investigation may result in fines of up to £1,000 being imposed.

Pregnancy

Pregnancy is currently accepted as a reason for dismissal only if you fail to carry out your job satisfactorily or if your continued employment would break a law and no other suitable post was available.

As and from October 1994 (European Union Pregnancy Directive) it will be unlawful to dismiss you by reason of pregnancy and the onus of proof will be on the employer to prove that the dismissal was not wholly or mainly owing to your pregnancy.

On maternity leave

You cannot be dismissed while on maternity leave nor can you be made redundant nor can notice of termination of your employment for any other reason be served.

Immediate cover

Remember you do not need 365 days' service to be covered against dismissal because of your pregnancy.

Probation

These periods are normally outside the scope of the Act where:

❏ there is a written contract
❏ the period of probation is a year or less and this is stated in the written contract
except where the dismissal results wholly or mainly from pregnancy or trade union activity.

Reasons for dismissal

The reasons for your dismissal must be given to you in writing *within fourteen days* of your having made the request. However, the employer can add other grounds when the case is heard by the Employment Appeals Tribunal or a Rights Commissioner.

Redress	Redress for unfair dismissal – see Compensation, above.
Redundancy	Selection criteria for redundancy must conform with any existing agreement on the matter and must be fair. For example, if you are made redundant and another worker doing the same or similar work as yourself, but with less service with the company than you, is kept on, this may be an unfair dismissal on the basis of unfair selection for redundancy.
Re-employment	If you are dismissed and rehired *within twenty-six weeks* this means your service is unbroken where the dismissal was wholly or partially intended to deprive you of rights under the Unfair Dismissals Act.
Series of contracts	Where there is no more than three months' 'break of service' between any two fixed term or specific purpose contracts, your service may be taken as 'continuous', i.e. unbroken, where either the Rights Commissioner, the Employment Appeals Tribunal or the Circuit Court so find.
Strikes	Strikes or lock-outs cannot be used to justify your dismissal:
	❏ where other workers involved in the same dispute are not let go, *or* ❏ where other workers are let go and later are taken back.
Time limit	The time limit for lodging your claim of unfair dismissal is normally *six months* from the date of dismissal. However, the Rights Commissioner or the Employment Appeals Tribunal may, in exceptional circumstances,

allow a case be heard where it is lodged *within twelve months* of the date of dismissal. Failure to take your case within six or in some cases twelve months means you lose your right to take a case under the Unfair Dismissals Act. You could still, however, use the Labour Relations Commission, Labour Court or the law courts.

Trade union activity

You may have reason to believe that you have been dismissed owing to your trade union activity. Trade union activity ranges from being an active member or union representative in your workplace to merely joining or proposing to join a union. If you believe that you have been sacked because of 'trade union activity' there are some important points you need to remember:

❏ you do not need to have worked for more than 365 days with the employer. The Unfair Dismissals Acts cover you from day one in respect of this type of dismissal
❏ your age does not affect your rights
❏ probationers, student nurses etc., are covered
❏ the burden of proving that the dismissal was owing to trade union activity rests with you, *not your employer.*

Unfair dismissal

Unfair dismissals take place when the employer fails to prove a case against you in respect of your ability, qualifications or conduct, or fails to prove that your redundancy was necessary or that the law required your dismissal. Other examples of unfair dismissals would be where the employer dismisses a worker wholly or mainly because of:

- ❑ age
- ❑ trade union activity
- ❑ political or religious views
- ❑ pregnancy
- ❑ taking a legal case or being a witness against the employer
- ❑ race or colour
- ❑ unfair selection for redundancy
- ❑ membership of the travelling community
- ❑ sexual orientation.

In deciding on the unfairness or otherwise of a case, the tribunal or Rights Commissioner is entitled to take any of the following into consideration:

- ❑ the reasonableness or otherwise of the employer's conduct in relation to your dismissal and whether or not that conduct contributed to the dismissal
- ❑ any failure to comply with disciplinary procedures or codes of practice.

Warnings of disciplinary action

Warnings of possible disciplinary action against you must normally be given before the action is imposed so that you have a chance to correct your ways. Before a dismissal takes place you would:

- ❑ normally have received two verbal and one written warnings. (The warnings should be clear and unambiguous. You should be in no doubt but that failure to comply with the reasonable requests of your employer *will* lead to dismissal.)
- ❑ normally have been given a reasonable period of time to prepare and make a defence
- ❑ have been given the opportunity of being represented either by your trade union or a friend.

WORKER PARTICIPATION (STATE ENTERPRISES) ACTS 1977–1993

Purpose

To allow workers in certain state enterprises to elect directly from among the workforce up to one third of the membership of the particular board of directors *and* to provide for sub-board level worker participation.

Who is covered

You are covered if you are over eighteen years of age and have been employed for at least one year, on a full-time or regular part-time basis, by one of the following designated state enterprises:

Board and sub-board participation

Aer Lingus Group plc, Aer Rianta, An Post, Bord na Móna, CIE, ESB, NET, NRB, Telecom Éireann.

Sub-board only

An Foras Áiseanna Saothair, Blood Transfusion Services Board, Board for the Employment of the Blind, Bord Fáilte, Bord Gáis, An Bord Tráchtála, BIM, Bus Éireann, Bus Átha Cliath, Central Fisheries Board, CERT, Dublin District Milk Board, Forbairt, Forfás, General Medical Services (Payments) Board, Great Southern Hotels, Hospital Joint Services Board, Iarnród Éireann, IDA, National Stud, Irish Steel, Kilkenny Design, Racing Board, RTÉ, Shannon Free Airport Development Company, Teagasc, Údarás na Gaeltachta and VHI.

DETAILS AND DEFINITIONS

Candidates

Candidates must be employed by the enterprise and be not less than eighteen and not more than sixty-five years of age on a date ('stated day') specified by the returning officer and must have worked for the company for a continuous period of at least three years.

Entitlement to seats

Up to one third of the seats on the board of the particular company can be allocated as worker director seats.

Fees

Fees, expenses etc. paid to other directors shall also be paid to worker directors.

Nominations

Nomination of candidates may be made by any qualified body of workers such as a trade union or other group which is accepted by the enterprise for collective bargaining purposes.

Period of office

The period of office of worker directors is three years, or equates with any other period of office held by other directors.

Postponement

Postponement of an election for worker directors, for a period of four years, may take place where a qualified body or bodies representing not less than 15 per cent of the workforce make such a written request to the returning officer *within seven days* of the 'stated day'. This request must be supported by a majority of those voting in a preliminary poll.

Returning officer

The returning officer is either the secretary of the designated body or any other person whom the secretary considers capable of doing the job and is acceptable to the majority of the workforce.

Sub-board participation

This level of participation involves at least the following:

❏ a regular exchange of views
❏ the provision in good time of information likely to have a significant effect on the employees
❏ the installation of an information system direct to each employee.

Appropriate officer

Each state body must appoint an 'appropriate officer' who will have the responsibility of overseeing the procedures for the establishment of sub-board participation. This officer may be the secretary of the enterprise or company, or any person appointed by the secretary who is acceptable to the employees, or any person appointed by the secretary.

Initiating the process

There are three ways in which sub-board participation can be put in place:

❏ through a request to the 'appropriate officer' on behalf of employee representative bodies who individually or collectively represent the majority of employees
❏ through a petition to the 'appropriate officer' by the majority of employees
❏ through a ballot of the employees. This requires that the 'appropriate officer' must have received an application for sub-board participation from at least 15 per cent of the employees. Should the ballot reject the proposal then no further ballot can be held for at least four years.

Vacancies

If vacancies arise for a worker director(s) they will be filled by the responsible minister who will have regard to the results of the most recent worker director election.

Voting

Voting is carried out by a single transferable vote, i.e. proportional representation, similar to that used in Dáil elections.

WORKER PROTECTION (REGULAR PART-TIME EMPLOYEES) ACT 1991

Purpose

To extend existing labour legislation to cover certain part-time workers.

Who is covered

You are covered if you are a part-time employee who is normally expected to work for at least eight hours per week and for at least thirteen weeks for the same employer.

DETAILS AND DEFINITIONS

Acts

The Acts whose cover has now been extended to apply to part-time workers are:

❏ Unfair Dismissals Acts 1977–1993
❏ Holiday (Employees) Acts 1973, 1991
❏ Minimum Notice and Terms of Employment Acts 1973–1991
❏ Maternity (Protection of Employees) Acts 1981, 1991
❏ Redundancy Payment Acts 1967–1991
❏ Protection of Employees (Employers' Insolvency) Acts 1984–1991
❏ Worker Participation (State Enterprises) Acts 1977–1993

Other legislation, e.g. Employment Equality Act, Safety, Health and Welfare at Work Act, Anti-Discrimination (Pay) Act, Payment of Wages Act, Terms of Employment (Information) Act, continues to cover part-time workers.

NB For more detail on each of the above Acts consult the relevant sections in this book.

Contracts

Contracts and information on a contract of employment should include such matters as pay, overtime, hours of work, shift rates, starting date, holidays, pension and sick pay etc. The Unfair Dismissals Act requires that you be given details of discipline procedures.

You are entitled to receive these terms of employment if you have completed four weeks x eight hours per week service with the same employer. Current employees are entitled to written terms of employment within one month of making a request and all new employees should automatically be issued with these within a month of starting work.

Disputes

Disputes regarding rights under this Act can be handled by you directly with your employer, or by your trade union. If the matter is not settled it can be referred to the Employment Appeals Tribunal.

Holiday entitlement

Holiday entitlement is six hours' paid leave for each hundred hours worked. Part-time employees are also entitled to public holidays (see Holiday Employees Act).

Insolvency Act

This Act provides cover after service of at least thirteen weeks x eight hours per week with the same employer. The Act sets out limited compensation for the following situations:

❏ up to eight weeks' loss of pay, sick pay, holiday pay
❏ certain awards from the law courts, Labour Court, Labour Relations Commission, Employment Appeals Tribunal, Employment Regulation Orders etc., covering such matters as equal pay, equality, unfair dismissal, minimum notice, minimum pay
❏ unpaid pension contributions.

All of the above are subject to financial limits, time constraints (within eighteen months before the date of insolvency) and to no appeals being outstanding in respect of equality legislation or unfair dismissal.

Maternity leave

You are entitled to maternity leave, ante and post-natal visits during working hours and to return to your job after maternity leave provided you have worked for the same employer for at least thirteen weeks x eight hours per week.

Maximum amount

The Maternity (Protection of Employees) Act gives you the right to at least eighteen weeks' maternity leave (maximum of twenty-two weeks in certain circumstances).

Social welfare

The Act does not give you the right to maternity leave payment. Payment is provided under the social welfare Acts if you have thirty-nine weeks' 'A 1' contributions.

Minimum notice

Minimum Notice and Terms of Employment Act applies after the completion of thirteen weeks x eight hours per week. The Act provides two rights:

❏ notice of termination or money in lieu
❏ written information about your terms of employment.

You should also consult the Terms of Employment (Information) Act 1994 about notice.

Notice of termination

Notice of termination of your employment must be given in accordance with the schedule set out below either in terms of time or money in lieu.

+ 13 weeks' to 2 years' service = 1 week's notice
+ 2 years' to 5 years' service = 2 weeks' notice
+ 5 years' to 10 years' service = 4 weeks' notice
+ 10 years' to 15 years' service = 6 weeks' notice
+ 15 years' service = 8 weeks' notice

Worker participation

Participation in the election of worker directors in certain state companies, e.g. ESB, Aer Lingus plc, Aer Rianta, CIE etc., is now extended to part-time workers covered by this Act.

Reductions

Reduction in your hours of work or in the number of continuous weeks you are employed by one employer is illegal where the intention of the reduction is to prevent you from being covered by the Act.

For example, it is illegal for your employer to let you go after twelve weeks or allow you work only seven hours in the thirteenth week or any other such variation designed to prevent you from being covered by the Act, *unless* your employer can prove that the reduction in hours was for some other lawful reason.

Redundancy

If you have thirteen weeks x eight hours per week x two years' service the Redundancy Payments Act provides monetary compensation for the loss of your job on the basis of:

❏ one half week's pay for each year of service under age forty-one
❏ plus one week's pay for each year of service over age forty-one
❏ plus one week's pay.

Re-hired

If you are re-hired within twenty-six weeks of being let go by the same employer your service is continuous for the purpose of deciding whether or not you are covered by the various Acts, provided the original dismissal was for the purpose of denying you your rights under this Act.

Unfair dismissal

The Unfair Dismissals Act applies after thirteen weeks x eight hours x one year's service with the same employer. However, if you are dismissed because of matters wholly or mainly related to your pregnancy or because of trade union activity, the Unfair Dismissals Act covers you from your first day of employment.

PART TWO

THE JOINT LABOUR COMMITTEES

SUMMARY OF THE JOINT LABOUR COMMITTEES (JLCs)

The purpose of Joint Labour Committees (JLCs) is to provide workers in certain occupations with basic minimum conditions of employment such as pay, hours of work, overtime, annual leave etc. Some Joint Labour Committees (JLCs) have a geographical limitation. For example, contract cleaning (at time of publication) is limited to Dublin city and county.

The committees meet at national level. Apart from the independent chair, the committees consist of employer and trade union representatives who agree, through a process of negotiation, the minimum pay and conditions and the time frame for which these will apply.

The committees issue Employment Regulation Orders (EROs). It is important to remember that these Employment Regulation Orders (EROs) establish *minimum* conditions. There is nothing to prevent an employer paying more or providing better conditions. This is the case in many companies where union organisation or the financial position of the company is strong.

The Employment Regulation Orders (EROs) are up-dated from time to time. The most up-to-date information can be obtained by telephoning or writing to:

Joint Labour Committees Section
The Labour Court
Tom Johnson House
Haddington Road
Dublin 4
Telephone (01) 660 8444

Titles of the Joint Labour Committees, services or industries included

Aerated Waters and Wholesale Bottling	Liquors Bottle filling Bottle washing Mineral waters Non-alcoholic drinks
Agricultural Workers	Agriculture Farming Horticulture Rearing, training, caring for animals Market gardening Sports grounds Private gardening Forestry
Brush and Broom	Brooms Brushes
Catering (excluding Dublin & Dún Laoghaire)*	Catering Cooking Waitressing Bar staff Clerical worker Pubs, in certain circumstances Fish and Chips

*A Catering Joint Labour Committee covering Dublin and Dún Laoghaire is expected to have effect during 1994.

Contract Cleaning (City & County of Dublin)	Contract cleaning
Hairdressing (Cork)	Hairdressing
Hairdressing (Dublin and Dún Laoghaire)	Manicuring
	Receptionist
	Beautician
Handkerchief and Household Piece Goods	Handkerchief
	Household piece goods
Hotels	Hotels
	Porters
	Cooking
	Waitressing
	Bar staff
	Clerical Work
Law Clerks	Law clerk
	Managing clerk
	Conveyancing clerk
	Cost clerk
	General law clerk
	Shorthand typist
	Typist
	Messenger
Provender Milling	Provender milling
	Animal feeds
Retail Grocery and Allied Trades	General retail sales
Shirtmaking	Shirtmaking
	Cutters
	Homeworkers
	Outworkers
	General workers
Tailoring	Tailoring
Women's Clothing and Millinery	Women's clothing

AERATED WATERS AND WHOLESALE BOTTLING JOINT LABOUR COMMITTEE (JLC)

Purpose

To provide workers with basic *minimum* conditions of employment, such as pay, hours of work, overtime, holidays etc.

Who is covered

You are covered if you are employed anywhere in the state in the manufacture of non-alcoholic drinks as well as liquors or in bottle washing and filling as specified under The Aerated Waters and Wholesale Bottling Trade (see 'No cover' and 'Type of operation' below).

DETAILS AND DEFINITIONS

Disputes

Disputes about any aspect of this Employment Regulation Order, including pay or conditions, can be dealt with directly by you, by your trade union, by the Joint Labour Committees Section of the Labour Court or by the Labour Inspectorate at the Department of Enterprise and Employment.

Employment Regulation Orders (EROs)

Employment Regulation Orders (EROs) are issued by the Joint Labour Committees following negotiation and agreement between trade unions and employers. They contain all aspects of your pay and conditions of employment and *must be displayed* in your workplace.

As aspects of the regulations, particularly pay rates, can vary from year to year, you should obtain a current Employment

Regulation Order for your employment from:
Joint Labour Committees Section
The Labour Court
Tom Johnson House
Haddington Road
Dublin 4
Telephone (01) 660 8444

Failure or refusal   Failure or refusal on the part of the employer
to:

❑ pay the rates set down, *or*
❑ comply with the conditions regarding
hours, overtime rates, holidays etc., *or*
❑ maintain records for three years on each
employee regarding pay, hours of work etc.,
or
❑ display the Employment Regulation Order
can result in the employer having to
compensate you for the loss suffered. In
addition the employer can be fined up to
£750 per offence.

Holidays   You are entitled to twenty days' annual leave
per year plus nine public holidays, calculated
in accordance with the Holiday (Employees)
Act.

Hours of work   Your hours of work are set at thirty-nine per
week. The Protection of Young Persons
(Employment) Act applies.

No cover   You are *not* covered by this JLC in the
following situations:

❑ where there is an agreement between a
trade union and an employer, or
representatives of a Joint Industrial Council,
regarding pay and conditions of a group of
workers

❏ where bottling operations are taking place on a licensed premises of a brewer or manufacturer of cider.

Overtime rates

Overtime rates are contained in the Employment Regulation Order and at time of publication were as follows:

❏ hours in excess of thirty-nine – time and a half
❏ Sunday, customary or public holidays – double time
❏ other rest days – first four hours at time and a half, with the remainder at double time.

The Protection of Young Persons (Employment) Act applies.

Pay rates

Pay rates are set out in the Employment Regulation Order. As these vary from time to time it is essential that you consult the most up-to-date version which can be obtained from the Joint Labour Committees Section of The Labour Court. The June 1993 ERO set the rate for an adult working a basic thirty-nine hour week at £145.18. The expected review date for this ERO is June 1994.

Remember you have a legal right to be paid these minimum rates.

Pension

A pension scheme providing for 50 per cent of final pensionable salary at age sixty-five provided you have forty years service is included in the Employment Regulation Order (ERO). Full-time permanent employees of twenty-five years of age or older who have at least two continuous years' service with the same employer are

| | eligible for membership of this scheme. |
| **Death in service** | Dependants of a member of the scheme, should the member die in service, are entitled to a death benefit of one and a half year's pay. |

Records

Records of the pay and hours of work of each employee covered by this Joint Labour Committee must be maintained for at least three years and be available for inspection (see 'Failure' above).

Service pay

Service pay is provided as follows:

❏ after five years – £0.50 per week
❏ after ten years – £1.00 per week
❏ after fifteen years – £1.50 per week
❏ after twenty years – £2.00 per week.

Type of operation

The types of operation covered by this Joint Labour Committee are:

❏ the manufacture or brewing of aerated waters, brewed liquors, cordials (non-alcoholic), flavoured syrups, unfermented sweet drinks and other similar beverages
❏ bottle washing, bottling and filling of the above drinks in bottles, casks, jars or siphons or other receptacles
❏ bottle washing, bottling and filling of receptacles with ale, stout, porter, other alcoholic beers and cider.

AGRICULTURAL WORKERS JOINT LABOUR COMMITTEE (JLC)

Purpose

To provide workers with basic *minimum* conditions of employment, such as pay, hours of work, overtime, holidays etc.

Who is covered

You are covered if you work in agriculture anywhere within the state (see 'Agriculture', 'Agricultural worker' and 'No cover' below).

DETAILS AND DEFINITIONS

Agriculture

Agriculture is defined in this Joint Labour Committee as any one or all of the following:

❏ caring, rearing or training of animals
❏ dairy farming
❏ horticulture
❏ land use in respect of grazing, market gardens, meadow, nursery grounds, orchards, osier, pasture, private gardens, sports grounds
❏ production of consumable produce
❏ poultry farming
and any other activity connected with agriculture.

Agricultural employer and agricultural worker

Agricultural employer and agricultural worker are defined in this Joint Labour Committee as follows:

❏ agricultural employer: someone who employs other persons as agricultural workers

❏ agricultural worker: someone who is employed under a contract of service or apprenticeship if their work is in agriculture.

Board and lodging

A deduction for board and lodging (house or cottage with or without garden) and the supply of milk may be made when calculating wages. These deductions are set out in the Employment Regulation Order, a copy of which you should obtain.

Disputes

Disputes about any aspect of the Employment Regulation Order, including pay or conditions, can be dealt with directly by you, by your trade union, by the Joint Labour Committees Section of the Labour Court or by the Labour Inspectorate at the Department of Enterprise and Employment.

Employment Regulation Orders (EROs)

Employment Regulation Orders (EROs) are issued by the Joint Labour Committees following negotiation and agreement between trade unions and employers. They cover all aspects of your pay and conditions of employment and *must be displayed* in your workplace.

As aspects of the regulations, particularly pay rates, can vary from year to year, you should obtain a current Employment Regulation Order for your employment from:

Joint Labour Committees Section
The Labour Court
Tom Johnson House
Haddington Road
Dublin 4
Telephone (01) 660 8444

Failure or refusal

Failure or refusal on the part of the employer to:

❏ pay the rates set down, *or*
❏ comply with the conditions regarding hours, overtime rates, holidays etc., *or*
❏ maintain records for three years on each employee regarding pay, hours of work etc., *or*
❏ display the Employment Regulation Order can result in the employer having to compensate you for the loss suffered. In addition the employer can be fined up to £750 per offence.

Holidays

You are entitled to twenty days' annual leave per year plus nine public holidays, calculated in accordance with the Holiday (Employees) Act 1973.

Hours of work

Your hours of work may be any one of the following:

❏ thirty-nine hours per week all year, *or*
❏ six months at thirty-eight hours per week followed by six months at forty hours per week, *or*
❏ three months at thirty-six hours per week with the balance of the year at forty hours per week.

The Protection of Young Persons (Employment) Act applies.

No cover

You are not covered by this Joint Labour Committee in the following situations:

❏ where you are employed in the mushroom growing industry and your pay and conditions are covered by a Registered Employment Agreement

❏ where you are employed as a groom and your pay and conditions are set by a Registered Employment Agreement
❏ where the work you are carrying out is mainly or wholly domestic service.

Overtime rates

Overtime rates are set out in the Employment Regulation Order and at time of publication are as follows:

❏ all hours worked in excess of the appropriate base (e.g. thirty-six, thirty-eight, thirty-nine or forty hours per week) will be paid at an hourly rate which shall be $1/39$th and a third of weekly wage
❏ all hours after 1 pm on Saturday, or a 'short day', will be at time and a third. A 'short day' is defined as a Saturday unless otherwise agreed
❏ all hours worked on a Sunday will be at time and two thirds.

Pay rates

Pay rates are set out in the Employment Regulation Order. As these vary from time to time it is essential that you consult the most up-to-date version which can be obtained from the Joint Labour Committees Section of The Labour Court. Remember you have a legal right to be paid these minimum rates. The pay rates, at time of publication, for adults working a basic thirty-nine hour week are:

❏ for those employed for less than five months – £137.24
❏ for those employed for more than five months – £148.90

This ERO was issued in March 1994; the expected review date is March 1995.

Records   Records of the pay and hours of work of each employee covered by this Joint Labour Committee must be maintained for at least three years and be available for inspection (see 'Failure' above).

BRUSH AND BROOM JOINT LABOUR COMMITTEE (JLC)

Purpose   To provide workers with basic *minimum* conditions of employment, such as pay, hours of work, overtime, holidays etc.

Who is covered   You are covered if you are employed anywhere in the state in the manufacture of brooms and brushes and associated finishing processes. This area of manufacture includes: brushes and brooms to be used for art, medicine, painting, white-wash, tar and any other brush or broom not specified (see 'No cover' and 'Type' below).

DETAILS AND DEFINITIONS

Compassionate leave   You are entitled to three days' compassionate leave in respect of the death of father, mother, sister, brother, son, daughter, husband or wife.

Death-in-service   Death-in-service benefit is payable and currently provides:

❏ £1,000 to an employee of twenty-five to sixty-five years of age
❏ £2,000 to an employee over sixty-five years of age.

These amounts are payable to the estate of any deceased worker who was twenty-five years of age or more and who had over three years' service with the employer at the time of death.

Disputes

Disputes about any aspect of this Employment Regulation Order, including pay or conditions, can be dealt with directly by you, by your trade union, by the Joint Labour Committees Section of the Labour Court or by the Labour Inspectorate at the Department of Enterprise and Employment.

Employment Regulation Orders (EROs)

Employment Regulation Orders (EROs) are issued by the Joint Labour Committees following negotiation and agreement between trade unions and employers. They cover all aspects of your pay and conditions of employment and *must be displayed* in your workplace.
As aspects of the regulations, particularly pay rates, can vary from year to year, you should obtain a current Employment Regulation Order for your employment from:

Joint Labour Committees Section
The Labour Court
Tom Johnson House
Haddington Road
Dublin 4
Telephone (01) 660 8444

Failure or refusal

Failure or refusal on the part of the employer to:

❏ pay the rates set down, *or*
❏ comply with the conditions regarding hours, overtime rates, holidays etc., *or*
❏ maintain records for three years on each employee regarding pay, hours of work etc., *or*
❏ display the Employment Regulation Order

can result in the employer having to compensate you for the loss suffered. In addition the employer can be fined up to £750 per offence.

Holidays

You are entitled to twenty days' annual leave per year plus nine public holidays calculated in accordance with the Holiday (Employees) Act 1973.

Hours of work

Your hours of work are set at thirty-nine per week. The Protection of Young Persons (Employment) Act applies.

No cover

You are not covered by this Joint Labour Committee if you are employed in the manufacture of feather brushes.

Overtime rates

These rates are contained in the Employment Regulation Order and at time of publication were as follows:

❏ hours in excess of thirty-nine per week or eight per day – time and a half
❏ hours on Saturday or a 'short day' – first four hours at time and a half, with the remainder at double time
❏ hours on Sunday, customary or public holiday – double time
❏ prior to normal starting time on a Monday – time and a half.

The Protection of Young Persons (Employment) Act applies.

Pay rates	Pay rates, piece rates and waiting time rates for all adult, learner, juvenile and piece-rate workers are as set out in the Employment Regulation Order. As these vary from time to time it is essential that you consult the most up-to-date version which can be obtained from the Joint Labour Committees Section of The Labour Court. The rates of pay, at time of publication, for adults working a basic thirty-nine hour week are £115.05 – £147.42 depending on the type of work performed.
	This ERO was issued in August 1991; no date has been set for a review.
	Remember you have a legal right to be paid these minimum rates.
Pension	A pension scheme is set out in the Employment Regulation Order and subject to certain conditions it currently provides a pension of £9 per week.
Records	Records of the pay and hours of work of each employee covered by this Joint Labour Committee must be maintained for at least three years and be available for inspection (see 'Failure' above).
Service pay	Service pay is provided for and is currently as follows:

❏ after five years – £0.50 per week
❏ after ten years – £1.00 per week
❏ after fifteen years – £1.50 per week
❏ after twenty years – £2.00 per week.

Sick pay	A sick pay scheme is set out in the Employment Regulation Order and currently provides, in certain circumstances, a payment of £10 per week.

Type of operation

The types of operation covered by this Joint Labour Committee in the making of brooms and brushes or associated processes include any or all of the following:

assembling; bleaching; bone, turning of; bone brush (cutting, drilling, fashioning and profiling); boring (by hand or machine); box-making; bunching; celluloid-working of, or celluloising; crimpling; cutting; drifting, dressing or cutting (of animal hair, bass, whisk or any other natural or synthetic fibre by hand or machine); dyeing; flirting; fork lifting; ivory, working of; knurling; labelling; materials handling; 'Pan hairs'; sanding; setting; scraping; servicing; sorting; stamping; stitching; trimming; wood finishing by hand or machine; warehousing; winding; wrapping or shrink wrapping, and any other operations normally associated with the manufacture of brooms and brushes.

CATERING JOINT LABOUR COMMITTEE (JLC)

Purpose

To provide workers with basic *minimum* conditions of employment, such as pay, hours of work, overtime, holidays etc.

Who is covered

You are covered if you work in catering establishments anywhere in the state with the exception of the county borough of Dublin and the area of the former borough of Dún

Laoghaire. A general description of this area of activity includes preparation and/or service of food or drink and incidental work (see also 'No cover' below).

DETAILS AND DEFINITIONS

Apprenticeship ratios

These ratios are set at one trainee per one trained worker.

Board and lodging

Deductions from wages may be made in respect of board and lodging, subject to a maximum amount. Where there is a Class A cook the maximum deduction is reduced and is further reduced where there is a Class B cook or a fully qualified cook working as Class B. All the deductions referred to in this section are set out in the Employment Regulation Order.

Breaks

You are entitled to a fifteen minutes' break for every four-and-a-half hours worked, excluding main meal breaks.

Catering establishment

A catering establishment is defined as a location used for selling food or drink to customers for consumption on the premises and includes fish and chip shops as well as ice cream parlours.

Pubs

The definition includes licensed premises (pubs) which serve hot food for consumption on the premises.

Certificate of service

Your employer is obliged to provide you with a certificate of service when you are leaving your employment. The certificate should indicate your period of employment, average weekly hours and the job classification(s) involved.

Differentials

Differentials in pay rates apply to the following posts which carry extra responsibility:

❑ head cook
❑ second head cook
❑ head waitress/waiter
❑ second waitress/waiter
❑ head barmaid/barman
❑ second head barmaid/barman.

The differentials, which vary from time to time, are contained in the Employment Regulation Order.

Disputes

Disputes about any aspect of this Employment Regulation Order, including pay or conditions, can be dealt with directly by you, by your trade union, by the Joint Labour Committees Section of the Labour Court or by the Labour Inspectorate at the Department of Enterprise and Employment.

Employment Regulation Orders (EROs)

Employment Regulation Orders (EROs) are issued by the Joint Labour Committees following negotiation and agreement between trade unions and employers. They cover all aspects of your pay and conditions of employment and *must be displayed* in your workplace.

As aspects of the regulations, particularly pay rates, can vary from year to year, you should obtain a current Employment Regulation Order for your employment from:

Joint Labour Committees Section
The Labour Court
Tom Johnson House
Haddington Road, Dublin 4
Telephone (01) 660 8444

Failure or refusal	Failure or refusal on the part of the employer to:

❏ pay the rates set down, *or*
❏ comply with the conditions regarding hours, overtime rates, holidays etc., *or*
❏ maintain records for three years on each employee regarding pay, hours of work etc., *or*
❏ display the Employment Regulation Order can result in the employer having to compensate you for the loss suffered. In addition the employer can be fined up to £750 per offence.

Holidays

You are entitled to nineteen days' annual leave per year plus nine public holidays, calculated in accordance with the Holiday (Employees) Act 1973. Your employer is obliged to give you at least six weeks' notice of your having to take annual leave. If you work a number of public holidays, and are taking time off in lieu, these days may be taken consecutively.

Hours of work

Your hours of work will normally be a ten-day fortnight of seventy-eight hours if you are over the age of sixteen years (see also Protection of Young Persons (Employment) Act). These hours are, however, subject to change and it is best to obtain the current Employment Regulation Order.

No cover

You are *not* covered by this Joint Labour Committee in the following situations:

❏ where there is an agreement between a trade union and an employer
❏ where there is an agreement at a Joint Industrial Council between worker and employer representatives of the council

❏ where cover is provided by another Joint Labour Committee through an Employment Regulation Order.

Cover does not extend to:

❏ managers
❏ assistant managers
❏ trainee managers
❏ premises registered under the Hotels Register of the Tourist Traffic Acts 1939-1987
❏ licensed premises (pubs) with not less than ten rooms for sleeping accommodation for travellers.

Overtime rates

Overtime rates are as follows:

❏ hours over seventy-eight per fortnight – time and a half
❏ hours worked on day off – double time
❏ hours worked over rostered duty – time and a half
❏ hours worked after midnight – double time.

It is advisable to obtain the current Employment Regulation Order as the above rates may change. The Protection of Young Persons (Employment) Act applies.

Part-time

Part-time or casual workers are entitled to be paid on the basis of the full-time hourly rate. For example if the full-time hourly rate for thirty-nine hours is £4 per hour and you are a part-time or casual worker your correct wages are the actual number of hours worked multiplied by the hourly rate, e.g.

thirty-nine hour week
    @ £4 per hour   = £156 per week
twenty hour week
    @ £4 per hour   = £80 per week
eight-and-a-quarter hour
    week @ £4 per hour   = £33 per week.

Pay rates

Pay rates are set out in the Employment Regulation Order. As these vary from time to time it is essential that you consult the most up-to-date version which can be obtained from the Joint Labour Committees Section of The Labour Court. The rates of pay, at time of publication, for adults working a basic thirty-nine hour week are:

❑ cook – £157.04
❑ short order fast service cook – £141.23
❑ counter assistant – £141.23
❑ waiter/waitress – £123.08
❑ barman/barmaid – £131.74
❑ clerical worker – £134.39
❑ general worker – £141.23
❑ cleaner/wash-up – £131.74

This ERO was issued in August 1993; the expected review date is August 1994.

Remember you have a legal right to be paid these minimum rates.

Initial rate

Except where a certificate of service showing twelve months' experience with a different employer can be provided, an initial rate of 90 per cent of the full pay rate will apply.

Records

Records of the pay and hours of work of each employee covered by this Joint Labour Committee must be maintained for at least

	three years and be available for inspection (see 'Failure' above).

Service charge

Service charge, where it exists, must be paid weekly to barmaids/barmen, waiters/waitresses and counter assistants. Where the majority of these staff agree, up to 20 per cent of the total service charge can be distributed among other workers covered by this JLC.

Spread-over

Spread-over duty and finishing time controls are as follows:

❏ a maximum of twelve hours in any day
❏ a guarantee of one day per week with a maximum of eight hours spread-over or two days per week with a ten-hour maximum spread-over
❏ a minimum break of eight hours between finishing and starting times.

All workers under the age of eighteen are prohibited from working later than 10 pm on any night.

Sunday

Sunday-off entitlement is every second Sunday which is regarded as a day off.

Type of operation

Workers covered by this Joint Labour Committee include the following:

❏ barmaid/barman – someone with two years' service (including training periods) wholly or mainly involved in the serving of alcoholic, non-alcoholic drinks and ancillary duties
❏ cook – someone who has three years' service (including training periods) at cooking duties and is involved in the

preparation of food for serving to the public or staff

❏ counter assistant – someone preparing and/or serving food at a counter, plus ancillary duties

❏ cleaner/wash-up – someone wholly or mainly involved in cleaning or washing duties

❏ clerical worker – someone wholly or mainly involved with clerical, cashier, and/or receptionist duties

❏ general worker – someone wholly or mainly involved in one or more of the following:

- kitchen portering
- preliminary food preparation
- general duties not specified in the job descriptions of the other workers as set out in this section.

❏ short order/fast service cook – someone solely involved in the preparation and/or cooking of any one or combination of the following:

- chips
- beef burgers
- pizza
- pancakes
- snack foods

❏ waiter/waitress – someone with two years' service (including training periods) who is wholly or mainly involved in serving tables plus other ancillary duties.

CONTRACT CLEANING (CITY AND COUNTY OF DUBLIN) JOINT LABOUR COMMITTEE (JLC)

Purpose

To provide workers with basic *minimum* conditions of employment, such as pay, hours of work, overtime, holidays etc.

Who is covered

You are covered if you are employed in the city and county of Dublin in the cleaning (which includes janitorial services) of the interiors of factories, hospitals, school, shops, universities and other similar establishments (see also 'No cover' below).

DETAILS AND DEFINITIONS

Change of address

Your employer must give you at least five days' notice before changing the location of the registered company office.

Change of contractor

Where one contractor loses a contract and another takes it over then the new contractor is obliged to give full consideration to the employees who have lost their jobs. In other words the new employer should, if at all possible, re-hire the employees from the old contract.

Change of hours

Once your hours of work have been assigned they cannot be reduced unless your employer gives you four weeks' notice or four weeks' pay in lieu of notice.

Contract of employment

Your employer is obliged to provide you with written terms of employment within a month of starting work. The contract should include:

❏ PAYE number
❏ PRSI number
❏ date of starting work
❏ name and address of company
❏ weekly and hourly rate of pay
❏ bonus scheme (if any)
❏ travel payments
❏ hours of work for morning, evening and/or night
❏ shift hours and rates
❏ pension scheme, if applicable.

Contract cleaning

Contract cleaning is defined as the cleaning of premises such as offices, factories, hospitals, schools etc. on a contract basis.

Disciplinary procedures

Disciplinary and grievance procedures are set out in the Employment Regulation Order, a copy of which you should obtain.

Disputes

Disputes about any aspect of this Employment Regulation Order, including pay or conditions, can be dealt with directly by you, by your trade union, by the Joint Labour Committees Section of the Labour Court or by the Labour Inspectorate at the Department of Enterprise and Employment.

Employment Regulation Orders (EROs)

Employment Regulation Orders (EROs) are issued by the Joint Labour Committees following negotiation and agreement between trade unions and employers. They contain all aspects of your pay and conditions of employment and *must be displayed* in your workplace.

As aspects of the regulations, particularly pay rates, can vary from year to year, you should obtain a current Employment Regulation Order for your employment from:

Joint Labour Committees Section
The Labour Court
Tom Johnson House
Haddington Road
Dublin 4
Telephone (01) 660 8444

Failure or refusal

Failure or refusal on the part of the employer to:

❏ pay the rates set down, *or*
❏ comply with the conditions regarding hours, overtime rates, holidays etc., *or*
❏ maintain records for three years on each employee regarding pay, hours of work etc., *or*
❏ display the Employment Regulation Order can result in the employer having to compensate you for the loss suffered. In addition the employer can be fined up to £750 per offence.

Holidays

Holiday entitlement is thirteen days per year and is pro-rata where less than a full year has been worked, i.e. 1.08 days for each month worked. If you work 1,400 hours or more per annum or 120 hours per month you are entitled to eighteen days' annual leave. In addition, all workers covered by this Joint Labour Committee are entitled to nine public holidays *plus* Good Friday (see also Worker Protection (Regular Part-Time Employees) Act).

Information

Information must be given to the employees and their representatives on the following:

❏ the name of the contract employer
❏ the identity of the responsible authority of the place being cleaned
❏ the date of termination of the contract and any change to this date.

No cover

You are not covered by this Joint Labour Committee in the following situations:

❏ where there is an agreement between an employer and a trade union
❏ where there is an agreement between the worker and employer representatives of a Joint Industrial Council
❏ where cover is provided by another Joint Labour Committee through an Employment Regulation Order
❏ where workers are involved with external structural cleaning.

Pay rates

Pay rates are set out in the Employment Regulation Order. As these vary from time to time it is essential that you consult the most up-to-date version which can be obtained from the Joint Labour Committees Section of The Labour Court. At the time of publication the hourly rate was £3.52 per hour. This rate is expected to be reviewed in June 1994.

Remember you have a legal right to be paid these minimum rates.

Records

Records of the pay and hours of work of each employee covered by this Joint Labour Committee must be maintained for at least three years and be available for inspection (see 'Failure' above).

Sick pay

An optional sick pay scheme which will cost you 0.5 per cent of basic pay can provide up to 20 per cent of basic weekly pay for up to six weeks in any rolling year.

Sunday work

Sunday work is included in the calculation of holiday pay where it is regularly part of your roster or normal working week. Calculations are made on the basis of the average number of Sundays worked in the previous thirteen weeks immediately prior to the holiday period.

Tax and PRSI

Your employer must provide evidence of payments being made to the Revenue Commissioners and/or the Department of Social Welfare if requested by you or your union.

Travel allowance

A travel allowance is paid on a per shift basis where no transport is provided by the employer. This means that when you work more than one shift you are entitled to a travel allowance for each shift worked. At time of publication the allowance stood at £0.70.

Union contributions

On receipt of a written request your employer must make arrangements for the deduction of union contributions from you wages for payment to your trades union.

HAIRDRESSING (CORK) JOINT LABOUR COMMITTEE (JLC)

Purpose

To provide workers with basic *minimum* conditions of employment, such as pay, hours of work, overtime, holidays etc.

Who is covered

You are covered if you are employed in any hairdressing undertaking in the Cork county borough.

DETAILS AND DEFINITIONS

Apprentice

An apprentice is defined as a person who:

Definitions

❑ has not completed a period of apprenticeship
❑ has a certificate of registration as an apprentice or on whose behalf an application has been made
❑ in the opinion of the Joint Labour Committee is not qualified as a hairdresser and who is carrying out any of the operations set out in 'Type' below.

Probation

Where, in your first employment, you are employed as an apprentice for a period of more than three months, but without a certificate of registration, this period will be counted as part of your apprenticeship.

Transfers

Where you transfer from a Dublin salon to a Cork salon or *vice versa* your period of apprenticeship will be recognised as transferring with you.

Illness

Where you are absent because of illness for a continuous period of more than one month, the period in excess of one month may be added to your period of apprenticeship at the discretion of the JLC.

Ratios of apprentices	The ratios of apprentices to qualified staff in ladies and gents' hairdressing are as follows:
Ladies	❏ one apprentice to one hairdresser
Gents	❏ one apprentice to one or two hairdressers for the first apprentice and then one apprentice per two hairdressers.
Commission rates	These are set out in the Employment Regulation Order and at time of publication were 10 per cent.
Disputes	Disputes about any aspect of this Employment Regulation Order, including pay or conditions, can be dealt with directly by you, by your trade union, by the Joint Labour Committees Section of the Labour Court or by the Labour Inspectorate at the Department of Enterprise and Employment.
Employment Regulation Orders (EROs)	Employment Regulation Orders (EROs) are issued by the Joint Labour Committees following negotiation and agreement between trade unions and employers. They cover all aspects of your pay and conditions of employment and *must be displayed* in your workplace.

As aspects of the regulations, particularly pay rates, can vary from year to year, you should obtain a current Employment Regulation Order for your employment from:

Joint Labour Committees Section
The Labour Court
Tom Johnson House
Haddington Road, Dublin 4
Telephone (01) 660 8444

Failure or refusal Failure or refusal on the part of the employer to:

❑ pay the rates set down, *or*
❑ comply with the conditions regarding hours, overtime rates, holidays etc., *or*
❑ maintain records for three years on each employee regarding pay, hours of work etc., *or*
❑ display the Employment Regulation Order can result in the employer having to compensate you for the loss suffered. In addition the employer can be fined up to £750 per offence.

Hairdresser A hairdresser is defined in the Employment Regulation Order as a person employed in any of the operations described in 'Type' below who has completed an apprenticeship or who in the opinion of the Joint Labour Committee has in some other way qualified as a hairdresser.

Hairdressing undertaking A hairdressing undertaking is defined as any undertaking or any part of an undertaking which is wholly or mainly involved in hairdressing operations and any connected work.

Holidays Annual leave entitlement is twenty days per year, in addition to nine public holidays, calculated in accordance with the Holiday (Employees) Act 1973.

Hours of work Your hours of work are set at thirty-nine per week. The Protection of Young Persons (Employment) Act applies.

Manicurist A manicurist is defined as a person wholly or mainly involved in manicuring.

Overtime

Overtime rates at the time of publication were as follows:

❑ in excess of thirty-nine hours – time and a half
❑ in excess of eight hours in any day – time and a half
❑ Sunday and public holidays – double time.

The Protection of Young Persons (Employment) Act applies.

Pay rates

Pay rates in respect of apprentices, hairdressers, manicurists and receptionists are included in the Employment Regulation Order. As these vary from time to time, it is essential that you consult the most up-to-date version which can be obtained from the Joint Labour Committees Section of the Labour Court. The rates of pay, at time of publication, for an adult worker on a basic thirty-nine hour week are:

❑ ladies' and unisex hairdressers £108.42 (March 1994), £112.67 (October 1994), £118.42 (June 1995)
❑ gents' hairdresser £126.02 (March 1994), £130.27 (October 1994), £136.02 (June 1995)
❑ manicurists £105.70 (March 1994), £109.94 (October 1994), £115.70 (June 1995)
❑ receptionists £112.12 (March 1994), £115.77 (October 1994), £121.12 (June 1995).

This ERO was issued in March 1994; the expected review date is June 1996.

Records

Records of the pay and hours of work of each employee covered by this Joint Labour Committee must be maintained for at least three years and be available for inspection (see 'Failure' above).

Service pay Service pay is as follows:

❑ after five years' service – 50p per week
❑ after ten years' service – 75p per week
❑ after fifteen years' service – £1.50 per week
❑ after twenty years' service – £2 per week

Type of operation The Employment Regulation Order covers the following operations when carried out on hair growing on the face, head or neck of males and females: bleaching, cutting, dressing, dyeing, lathering, setting, shampooing, shaving or other similar operations.

HAIRDRESSING (DUBLIN AND DÚN LAOGHAIRE) JOINT LABOUR COMMITTEE (JLC)

Purpose To provide workers with basic *minimum* conditions of employment, such as pay, hours of work, overtime, holidays etc.

Who is covered You are covered if you are working in any hairdressing undertaking in the county borough of Dublin, the area of the former borough of Dún Laoghaire and the urban district of Bray.

DETAILS AND DEFINITIONS

Apprentice

An apprentice is defined as a person who:

Definitions

❑ has not completed a period of apprenticeship
❑ has a certificate of registration as an apprentice or on whose behalf an application has been made
❑ in the opinion of the Joint Labour Committee is not qualified as a hairdresser and who is carrying out any of the operations set out in 'Type' below.

Probation

Where, in your first employment, you are employed as an apprentice for a period of more than three months, but without a certificate of registration, this period will be counted as part of your apprenticeship.

Transfers

Where you transfer from a Dublin salon to a Cork salon or *vice versa* your period of apprenticeship will be recognised as transferring with you.

Illness

Where you are absent because of illness for a continuous period of more than one month, the period in excess of one month may be added to your period of apprenticeship at the discretion of the JLC.

Ratios of apprentices

The ratios of apprentices to qualified staff in ladies and gents' hairdressing are as follows:

Ladies
Gents

❑ one apprentice to one hairdresser
❑ one apprentice to one or two hairdressers for the first apprentice and then one apprentice per two hairdressers.

Beautician	A beautician is defined as a person wholly or mainly involved in the process of beauty culture.
Commission rates	Commission rates are set out in the Employment Regulation Order and at time of publication varied from 10 per cent to 12.5 per cent. From the point of view of calculating commission, 'takings' is understood to mean all takings other than those on the sales of proprietary items.
Compassionate leave	You are entitled to compassionate leave as follows:

❏ death of mother, father, sister, brother, wife, husband, son or daughter – three days
❏ death of aunt, uncle, parent-in-law, grandparent or other more distant relative – one day, by agreement with the employer. |
| **Disputes** | Disputes about any aspect of this Employment Regulation Order, including pay or conditions, can be dealt with directly by you, by your trade union, by the Joint Labour Committees Section of the Labour Court or by the Labour Inspectorate at the Department of Enterprise and Employment. |
| **Employment Regulation Orders (EROs)** | Employment Regulation Orders (EROs) are issued by the Joint Labour Committees following negotiation and agreement between trade unions and employers. They cover all aspects of your pay and conditions of employment and *must be displayed* in your workplace.

As aspects of the regulations, particularly pay rates, can vary from year to year, you should obtain a current Employment Regulation Order for your employment from: |

Joint Labour Committees Section
The Labour Court
Tom Johnson House
Haddington Road, Dublin 4
Telephone (01) 660 8444

Failure or refusal

Failure or refusal on the part of the employer to:

❏ pay the rates set down, *or*
❏ comply with the conditions regarding hours, overtime rates, holidays etc., *or*
❏ maintain records for three years on each employee regarding pay, hours of work etc., *or*
❏ display the Employment Regulation Order

can result in the employer having to compensate you for the loss suffered. In addition the employer can be fined up to £750 per offence.

Hairdresser

A hairdresser is defined as a person employed in any of the operations described in 'Type' below who has completed an apprenticeship or who in the opinion of the Joint Labour Committee has in some other way qualified as a hairdresser.

Hairdressing undertaking

A hairdressing undertaking is defined as any undertaking or any part of an undertaking which is wholly or mainly involved in hairdressing operations and any connected work.

Holidays

You are entitled to twenty days' annual leave per year plus nine public holidays, calculated in accordance with the Holiday (Employees) Act 1973.

Hours of work

Hours of work as set out in the Employment Regulation Order are thirty-nine per week with a maximum norm of eight hours in any one day. The Protection of Young Persons (Employment) Act applies.

Manicurist   A manicurist is defined as a person wholly or mainly involved in manicuring.

Overtime rates   Overtime rates at the time of publication were as follows:

❏ in excess of thirty-nine hours – time and a half
❏ in excess of eight hours in any day – time and a half
❏ Sunday and public holidays – double time.

The Protection of Young Persons (Employment) Act applies.

Pay rates   These rates in respect of apprentices, beauticians, hairdressers, manicurists, operatives and receptionists are included in the Employment Regulation Order. The up-to-date version can be obtained from the Joint Labour Committees Section of the Labour Court. The pay rates at time of publication, for an adult worker on a basic thirty-nine hour week are:

❏ ladies' hairdresser – £132.67
❏ gents' and unisex hairdresser – £134.67
❏ beautician/manicurist – £121.57

This ERO was issued in November 1993; the expected review date is November 1994.

Records   Records of the pay and hours of work of each employee covered by this Joint Labour Committee must be maintained for at least three years and be available for inspection (see 'Failure' above).

Service pay	Service pay at time of publication was as follows:
	❏ after five years – 50p per week ❏ after ten years – 75p per week ❏ after fifteen years – £1.50 per week ❏ after twenty years' continuous service – £2 per week.
Sick pay scheme	A sick pay scheme is provided for and is currently £8 per week, paid in certain circumstances. The stipulated contributions to the scheme are £0.10 for apprentices and £0.12 for qualified staff.
Type of operation	The Employment Regulation Order covers the following operations when carried out on hair growing on the face, head or neck of males and females: bleaching, cutting, dressing, dyeing, lathering, setting, shampooing, shaving, singeing, tinting, or other similar operations.

HANDKERCHIEF AND HOUSEHOLD PIECE GOODS JOINT LABOUR COMMITTEE (JLC)

Purpose	To provide workers with basic *minimum* conditions of employment, such as pay, hours of work, overtime, holidays etc.
Who is covered	You are covered if you are employed anywhere in the state in any branch of the

trade specified in the Trade Board (Handkerchief and Household Goods) Order 1935. A general description of this area of work is the making of handkerchiefs, bedclothes, furniture covers etc. from such material as cotton, linen, silk but excluding American oilcloth, paper or rubberised materials (see 'Type' below).

DETAILS AND DEFINITIONS

Disputes

Disputes about any aspect of this Employment Regulation Order, including pay or conditions, can be dealt with directly by you, by your trade union, by the Joint Labour Committees Section of the Labour Court or by the Labour Inspectorate at the Department of Enterprise and Employment.

Employment Regulation Orders (EROs)

Employment Regulation Orders (EROs) are issued by the Joint Labour Committees following negotiation and agreement between trade unions and employers. They cover all aspects of your pay and conditions of employment and *must be displayed* in your workplace.

As aspects of the regulations, particularly pay rates, can vary from year to year, you should obtain a current Employment Regulation Order for your employment from:

Joint Labour Committees Section
The Labour Court
Tom Johnson House
Haddington Road
Dublin 4
Telephone (01) 660 8444

Failure or refusal	Failure or refusal on the part of the employer to:

❏ pay the rates set down, *or*
❏ comply with the conditions regarding hours, overtime rates, holidays etc., *or*
❏ maintain records for three years on each employee regarding pay, hours of work etc., *or*
❏ display the Employment Regulation Order can result in the employer having to compensate you for the loss suffered. In addition the employer can be fined up to £750 per offence.

Holidays	You are entitled to twenty days per year in addition to nine public holidays. The Holiday (Employees) Act 1973 is used as the basis for applying the leave, calculating pay etc.

Hours of work	Your hours of work per week are specified at thirty-nine. The Protection of Young Persons (Employment) Act applies.

Learners	Generally speaking learners shall not exceed a ratio of two to every five workers. Details of the conditions attaching to learners' rates of pay, training, training certificates etc. are set out in the Employment Regulation Order.

Overtime rates	Overtime rates, at time of publication, are:

❏ all hours in excess of normal hours up to twelve noon on Saturday – time and a half
❏ all hours after twelve noon on Saturday and up to normal starting time on Monday morning – double time.

Pay rates	Rates covering minimum time rates, piece-work basis time rates and overtime rates are provided for in the Employment Regulation

Order. The most up-to-date version can be obtained from the Joint Labour Committees Section of the Labour Court. The pay rate at time of publication, for an adult worker on a basic thirty-nine hour week is £128.61, with a proposed increase to £131.18.

This ERO was issued in January 1993 and is currently under review.

Pension

The pension scheme in this Joint Labour Committee provides a pension of £4.00 per week after thirty years' service. Less than thirty years' service will attract a pension of 13p per year of service completed. A death-in-service benefit of £1,200 is also provided.

Records

Records of the pay and hours of work of each employee covered by this Joint Labour Committee must be maintained for at least three years and be available for inspection (see 'Failure' above).

Service pay

Service pay at time of publication was as follows:

❏ after five years – 50p per week
❏ after ten years – £1.00 per week
❏ after fifteen years – £1.50 per week
❏ after twenty years' continuous service – £2 per week.

Type of operation

The type of work covered by this Joint Labour Committee includes making of such items as bed linen, bed spreads, cushion covers, dusters, other similar household articles, handkerchiefs, mufflers, scarves, sideboard covers, tablenapery, table centres, tea-cloths, towels which involve any or all of the following operations:

❏ machine work covering – button holing, decorative needle work, embroidery, fancy machine, stitching, hemming, hem-stitching, nickelling, overlocking, paring, plain machine stitching, scalloping, spoking, tambouring, thread-clipping, thread-drawing, top sewing
❏ cutting etc. – cutting, hooking and/or tearing of materials
❏ finishing etc. – boxing, finishing, folding, laundering, ornamenting, packing, smoothing, warehousing or other similar operations connected with the making of the items specified above.

HOTELS JOINT LABOUR COMMITTEE (JLC)

Purpose

To provide workers with basic *minimum* conditions of employment, such as pay, hours of work, overtime, holidays etc.

Who is covered

You are covered if you are employed anywhere in the state in a hotel establishment except in the county boroughs of Dublin and Cork and the area of the former borough of Dún Laoghaire.

DETAILS AND DEFINITIONS

Breaks

Breaks from work are an entitlement and you do not have to work for more than four-and-a-half hours without a break of at least fifteen minutes, excluding main meal breaks.

The Protection of Young Persons
(Employment) Act also applies.

**Certification
of service**

Your employer is obliged to provide you with
a certificate of service when leaving your
employment. The certificate should indicate
your period of employment, average weekly
hours and the job classification(s) involved.

Disputes

Disputes about any aspect of this
Employment Regulation Order, including pay
or conditions, can be dealt with directly by
you, by your trade union, by the Joint Labour
Committees Section of the Labour Court or
by the Labour Inspectorate at the Department
of Enterprise and Employment.

**Employment
Regulation
Orders (EROs)**

Employment Regulation Orders (EROs) are
issued by the Joint Labour Committees
following negotiation and agreement between
trade unions and employers. They cover all
aspects of your pay and conditions of
employment and *must be displayed* in your
workplace.

As aspects of the regulations, particularly pay
rates, can vary from year to year, you should
obtain a current Employment Regulation
Order for your employment from:

Joint Labour Committees Section
The Labour Court
Tom Johnson House
Haddington Road
Dublin 4
Telephone (01) 660 8444

**Extra
responsibilities**

Certain posts attract additional payments and
these are set out in the Employment
Regulation Order. They include:

❏ head barmaid/barman and second head barmaid/barman
❏ head cook and second head cook
❏ head house assistant and second head house assistant
❏ head porter and second head porter
❏ head waiter/waitress and second head waiter/waitress.

Failure or refusal

Failure or refusal on the part of the employer to:

❏ pay the rates set down, *or*
❏ comply with the conditions regarding hours, overtime rates, holidays etc., *or*
❏ maintain records for three years on each employee regarding pay, hours of work etc., *or*
❏ display the Employment Regulation Order can result in the employer having to compensate you for the loss suffered. In addition the employer can be fined up to £750 per offence.

Finishing time

Finishing time is regulated as follows:
each week throughout the year – one early at 7 pm or two at 8.30 pm.
Workers under the age of eighteen years shall not be required to work later than 10 pm on any night.

Holidays

You are entitled to nineteen days' holidays per year in addition to the nine public holidays, applied on the basis of the Holiday (Employees) Act 1973.

Notice of at least six weeks must be given to the employee by the employer regarding the timing of annual leave.

Hotel

A hotel is defined in this Joint Labour Committee as:

❑ a premises registered in the Hotels Register under the Tourist Traffic Acts 1939 to 1987
❑ a premises licensed under the Licensing Acts 1833 to 1962 and having no less than ten rooms available for travellers' sleeping arrangements.

Hours of work

Hours of work are set out in the Employment Regulation Order and at time of publication were as follows:

❑ during the season, i.e. that period between the Sunday before Easter Sunday and the last Sunday in September, the normal working fortnight shall be seventy-eight hours in any ten days
❑ during the off-season the normal working fortnight shall be seventy-eight hours with alternate Sundays off.

The Protection of Young Persons (Employment) Act applies.

Night duty

If you work on night duty you are entitled to receive an allowance of 20 per cent of basic pay.

No cover

You are not covered by this Joint Labour Committee if you are employed as:

❑ assistant manager
❑ head storeperson
❑ housekeeper
❑ manager
❑ receptionist
❑ trainee manager, *or*
❑ if you are covered by another Registered Agreement.

Overtime rates

Overtime rates at time of publication were as follows:

❏ hours in excess of normal – time and a half
❏ Sunday work as part of the seventy-eight-hour roster – double time
❏ Sunday work in addition to the seventy-eight-hour roster – two additional days' pay.

The Protection of Young Persons (Employment) Act applies.

Pay rates

Rates (minimum) covering bar staff, cooks, house assistants, porters and general workers are as set out in the Employment Regulation Order. The most up-to-date version can be obtained from the Joint Labour Committees Section of the Labour Court. The pay rates take into account tipping and non-tipping zones and include guaranteed gratuities. The maximum amounts that may be deducted in respect of board and lodging are also included. The pay rates, at time of publication, for an adult working a basic thirty-nine hour week are:

❏ cook – £153.19
❏ general worker/barman/barmaid – £138.72
❏ waiter/waitress/porter – £128.95
❏ house assistant – £118.84
❏ page – £97.49

This ERO was issued in August 1993 and is currently under review.

Records

Records of the pay and hours of work of each employee covered by this Joint Labour Committee must be maintained for at least three years and be available for inspection (see 'Failure' above).

Spread-over

Spread-over duty is limited in the Employment Regulation Order to no more than fourteen hours in any day. A minimum period of eight hours free from work must be allowed between the normal finishing time and starting time the next morning.

Type of work A general description of the type of work covered by this Joint Labour Committee would include:

❏ office work
❏ preparation and/or serving of food and drink, and incidental work
❏ the provision of living accommodation, and incidental work
❏ the retail sale of goods, and incidental work
❏ store/warehouse work.

LAW CLERKS JOINT LABOUR COMMITTEE (JLC)

Purpose To provide workers with basic *minimum* conditions of employment, such as pay, hours of work, overtime, holidays etc.

Who is covered You are covered if you are employed anywhere in the state either whole-time or part-time by solicitors, bodies corporate or under the direction of law agents in the positions set out below (see 'Type' below).

DETAILS AND DEFINITIONS

Disputes

Disputes about any aspect of this Employment Regulation Order, including pay or conditions, can be dealt with directly by you, by your trade union, by the Joint Labour Committees Section of the Labour Court or by the Labour Inspectorate at the Department of Enterprise and Employment.

Employment Regulation Orders (EROs)

Employment Regulation Orders (EROs) are issued by the Joint Labour Committees following negotiation and agreement between trade unions and employers. They cover all aspects of your pay and conditions of employment and *must be displayed* in your workplace.

As aspects of the regulations, particularly pay rates, can vary from year to year, you should obtain a current Employment Regulation Order for your employment from:

Joint Labour Committees Section
The Labour Court
Tom Johnson House
Haddington Road
Dublin 4
Telephone (01) 660 8444

Failure or refusal

Failure or refusal on the part of the employer to:

❑ pay the rates set down, *or*
❑ comply with the conditions regarding hours, overtime rates, holidays etc., *or*
❑ maintain records for three years on each employee regarding pay, hours of work etc., *or*
❑ display the Employment Regulation Order can result in the employer having to compensate you for the loss suffered. In

addition the employer can be fined up to £750 per offence.

Holidays

You are entitled to twenty days' annual leave per year plus nine public holidays, calculated in accordance with the Holiday (Employees) Act 1973.

Hours of work

Your hours of work are thirty-eight per five-day week.

The Protection of Young Persons (Employment) Act applies.

Overtime rates

Overtime rates are set out in the Employment Regulation Order and at the time of publication were as follows:

❏ in excess of thirty-eight hours per week – time and a half
❏ On Sundays or public holidays – double time.

The Protection of Young Persons (Employment) Act applies.

Pay rates

Pay rates are covered by the Employment Regulation Order (see above) and cover all the categories listed in 'Type' below. The most up-to-date version can be obtained from the Joint Labour Committees Section of the Labour Court. The pay rates, at time of publication, for an adult working a basic thirty-eight hour week are:

❏ managing clerk – £222.50
❏ conveyancing and cost clerk – £197.63
❏ general law clerk – £113.80 to £185.20, over ten years
❏ shorthand typist – £113.80 to £170.28, over nine years

❏ messenger – £109.86 to £121.82, over three years.

This ERO was issued in August 1993; the expected review date is August 1994.

Records

Records of the pay and hours of work of each employee covered by this Joint Labour Committee must be maintained for at least three years and be available for inspection (see 'Failure' above).

Types of worker

The types of worker covered by this Joint Labour Committee are as follows:

❏ managing clerk – a legal assistant, fully experienced in all the facets of a solicitor's work, who regularly carries out interviews with clients without constant supervision
❏ conveyancing clerk – a person wholly or mainly involved in title work including preparation of contracts, investigation of title, drawing up and completion of conveyances, mortgages and other deeds
❏ cost clerk – a person wholly or mainly involved in the drawing up and taxation of the employer's costs. He/she is not paid on a commission basis
❏ general law clerk – a person other than those listed above, or a shorthand typist or typist, who may however be a court clerk, or book-keeper who is wholly or mainly involved with clerical or book-keeping duties
❏ shorthand typist or typist – a person wholly or mainly involved with one or more of the following duties: shorthand, typing, dictaphone, reception, copying, scrivenery, filing, dispatch, post and telephone operation
❏ messenger – a person wholly or mainly involved in post collection and delivery.

PROVENDER MILLING JOINT LABOUR COMMITTEE (JLC)

Purpose

To provide workers with basic *minimum* conditions of employment, such as pay, hours of work, overtime, holidays etc.

Who is covered

You are covered if you are employed anywhere in the state in the manufacture or packing of animal feed stuffs (see 'Type' and 'No cover' below).

DETAILS AND DEFINITIONS

Disputes

Disputes about any aspect of this Employment Regulation Order, including pay or conditions, can be dealt with directly by you, by your trade union, by the Joint Labour Committees Section of the Labour Court or by the Labour Inspectorate at the Department of Enterprise and Employment.

Employment Regulation Orders (EROs)

Employment Regulation Orders (EROs) are issued by the Joint Labour Committees following negotiation and agreement between trade unions and employers. They cover all aspects of your pay and conditions of employment and *must be displayed* in your workplace.

As aspects of the regulations, particularly pay rates, can vary from year to year, you should obtain a current Employment Regulation Order for your employment from:

Joint Labour Committees Section
The Labour Court

Tom Johnson House
Haddington Road
Dublin 4
Telephone (01) 660 8444

Failure or refusal

Failure or refusal on the part of the employer to:

❏ pay the rates set down, *or*
❏ comply with the conditions regarding hours, overtime rates, holidays etc., *or*
❏ maintain records for three years on each employee regarding pay, hours of work etc., *or*
❏ display the Employment Regulation Order can result in the employer having to compensate you for the loss suffered. In addition the employer can be fined up to £750 per offence.

Holidays

You are entitled to twenty days' annual leave per year plus nine public holidays calculated in accordance with the Holiday (Employees) Act 1973.

Hours of work

Your hours of work are set at thirty-nine per week.

The Protection of Young Persons (Employment) Act applies.

No cover

You are not covered by this Joint Labour Committee in the following situations or occupations:

❏ carters or lorry drivers
❏ production of animal foodstuffs by natural means or agencies
❏ production of animal foodstuffs during the course of ordinary farm husbandry.

Overtime rates	Overtime rates are contained in the Employment Regulation Order and at time of publication were as follows:

❏ hours in excess of thirty-nine – time and a half
❏ Sunday, customary or public holidays – double time
❏ other rest days – first four hours at time and a half, with the balance at double time.

The Protection of Young Persons (Employment) Act applies.

Pay rates

Pay rates are established in the Employment Regulation Order and cover you if you are over the age of sixteen. The most up-to-date version can be obtained from the Joint Labour Committees Section of the Labour Court. The pay rate for an adult working a basic thirty-nine hour week is £150.41.

This ERO was issued in June 1994. The expected review date is June 1995.

Pension

A pension scheme (contributory) providing 50 per cent of final pensionable salary is included in this Employment Regulation Order.

Records

Records of the pay and hours of work of each employee covered by this Joint Labour Committee must be maintained for at least three years and be available for inspection (see 'Failure' above).

Service pay

Pay at time of publication was as follows:

❏ after five years – 50p per week
❏ after ten years – £1.00 per week

□ after fifteen years – £1.50 per week
□ after twenty years – £2 per week.

Sick pay

A sick pay scheme is provided for under the Employment Regulation Order and is currently £6 per week in certain circumstances.

Type of work

A general description of this area of operations would include the manufacture of animal foodstuffs by any process including:

□ cutting of cereals
□ flaking of cereals
□ grinding of cereals
□ mixing of substances.

RETAIL GROCERY AND ALLIED TRADES JOINT LABOUR COMMITTEE (JLC)

Purpose

To provide workers with basic *minimum* conditions of employment, such as pay, hours of work, overtime, holidays etc.

Who is covered

You are covered if you are employed anywhere in the state in a company that is wholly or mainly involved in the retail, grocery and allied trades activities (see also 'No cover' below).

DETAILS AND DEFINITIONS

Breaks

You are entitled to at least fifteen minutes free from work when you have been continuously working for four-and-a-half hours, excluding main meal breaks.

Certificate of service

Your employer is obliged to provide you with a certificate of service when leaving your employment. The certificate should indicate your period of employment, average weekly hours and the job classification(s) involved.

Disputes

Disputes about any aspect of this Employment Regulation Order, including pay or conditions, can be dealt with directly by you, by your trade union, by the Joint Labour Committees Section of the Labour Court or by the Labour Inspectorate at the Department of Enterprise and Employment.

Employment Regulation Orders (EROs)

Employment Regulation Orders (EROs) are issued by the Joint Labour Committees following negotiation and agreement between trade unions and employers. They cover all aspects of your pay and conditions of employment and *must be displayed* in your workplace.

As aspects of the regulations, particularly pay rates, can vary from year to year, you should obtain a current Employment Regulation Order for your employment from:

Joint Labour Committees Section
The Labour Court
Tom Johnson House
Haddington Road
Dublin 4
Telephone (01) 660 8444

Extra responsibility	Responsiblility for the management of a shop or a department or the work of others should attract a differential of 7.5 per cent.
Failure or refusal	Failure or refusal on the part of the employer to:

❏ pay the rates set down, *or*
❏ comply with the conditions regarding hours, overtime rates, holidays etc., *or*
❏ maintain records for three years on each employee regarding pay, hours of work etc., *or*
❏ display the Employment Regulation Order can result in the employer having to compensate you for the loss suffered. In addition the employer can be fined up to £750 per offence.

Holidays	You are entitled to twenty days' annual leave per year plus nine public holidays calculated in accordance with the Holiday (Employees) Act 1973.
Hours of work	Hours of work are set out in the Employment Regulation Order (see above) and currently stand at thirty-nine per week. Any change in your normal rostered hours must be notified to you at least one week in advance of the proposed change.

The Protection of Young Persons (Employment) Act applies.

No cover	You are *not* covered by this Joint Labour Committee if you are:

❏ in any type of employment already covered by a different Joint Labour Committee or Employment Regulation Order

❏ in any type of employment where the rates of pay and conditions are no less favourable than those provided for in the current Regulation Order
❏ an assistant manager
❏ an apprentice beef butcher
❏ employed in an independent off-licence
❏ a manager
❏ employed in a shop selling only bread or confectionery.

Overtime rates

Overtime hours and the appropriate pay rates are set out in the Employment Regulation Order. At time of publication these were as follows:

Rates

❏ up to midnight (Monday to Saturday) – time and a half
❏ midnight to 7 am – double time
❏ Sunday as overtime – double time
❏ public holiday as overtime – double time.

Time off
in lieu

Time-off in lieu may apply only by agreement.

Change of
roster

Any change in normal rostered hours must be notified to the employee at least one week in advance of the change.

Pay rates

Pay rates are as set out in the Employment Regulation Order. The most up-to-date version can be obtained from the Joint Labour Committees Section of the Labour Court. The pay rates, at time of publication, for an adult working a basic thirty-nine hour week are:

❏ general sales assistant and clerical worker – £88.00 to £160.29 over seven years
❏ general ancillary worker – £81.51.

This ERO was issued in June 1994; the expected review date is June 1995.

Records

Records of the pay and hours of work of each employee covered by this Joint Labour Committee must be maintained for at least three years and be available for inspection (see 'Failure' above).

Type of work

A general description of the work involved would include the sale by retail of: bacon, bread, cigars, cigarettes, confectionery, sugar, chocolate, drink, ice cream, lighters, pressed beef, snuff, tobacco.

Unsocial hours

At time of publication the following rates apply to unsocial hours:

❏ midnight to 7am – 25 per cent premium
❏ Sunday – 33$\frac{1}{3}$ per cent premium.

SHIRTMAKING JOINT LABOUR COMMITTEE (JLC)

Purpose

To provide workers with basic *minimum* conditions of employment, such as pay, hours of work, overtime, holidays etc.

Who is covered

You are covered if you are employed anywhere in the state in any branch of the trade as specified in the Trade Boards (Shirtmaking) Order 1920. See 'Job definition', 'No cover' and 'Type' below.

DETAILS AND DEFINITIONS

Disputes

Disputes about any aspect of this Employment Regulation Order, including pay or conditions, can be dealt with directly by you, by your trade union, by the Joint Labour Committees Section of the Labour Court or by the Labour Inspectorate at the Department of Enterprise and Employment.

Employment Regulation Orders (EROs)

Employment Regulation Orders (EROs) are issued by the Joint Labour Committees following negotiation and agreement between trade unions and employers. They cover all aspects of your pay and conditions of employment and *must be displayed* in your workplace.

As aspects of the regulations, particularly pay rates, can vary from year to year, you should obtain a current Employment Regulation Order for your employment from:

Joint Labour Committees Section
The Labour Court
Tom Johnson House
Haddington Road
Dublin 4
Telephone (01) 660 8444

Failure or refusal

Failure or refusal on the part of the employer to:

❏ pay the rates set down, *or*
❏ comply with the conditions regarding hours, overtime rates, holidays etc., *or*
❏ maintain records for three years on each employee regarding pay, hours of work etc., *or*
❏ display the Employment Regulation Order can result in the employer having to compensate you for the loss suffered. In

addition the employer can be fined up to £750 per offence.

Holidays

You are entitled to twenty days' annual leave per year plus nine public holidays, calculated in accordance with the Holiday (Employees) Act 1973.

Hours of work

Your hours of work are established as thirty-nine per week.

The Protection of Young Persons (Employment) Act applies.

Job definition

The definitions or classes contained in the Employment Regulation Order are as follows:

❑ special or measure cutter (Job Class 1) – someone who has sufficient skill to be able to take a complete set of measures, cut from model patterns and alter patterns other than stock patterns

❑ cutter (Job Class 2) – someone wholly or mainly involved in cutting who has three years' experience in the trade

❑ general worker (Job Class 3) – someone carrying out functions requiring skill levels higher than those of Job Classes 4 and 5

❑ learner cutter – someone who is being instructed in any or all of the following: hooking-up, cutting, marking-out, folding, marking-in and dividing. The person will be registered or be in the process of being registered in accordance with the Joint Labour Committees' regulations

❑ home worker or out worker – someone who operates outside of premises controlled by the employer or his representative, e.g. a person's home

❏ special machinist (Job Class 4) – someone who operates a sewing machine to a high degree of accuracy and quality standard
❏ all other operations (Job Class 5) – someone employed on operations which do not require the skill level of Job Class 4 or higher. This person would be involved in controlled manual, semi-automatic and automatic operations.

Learners

Learners are covered by this Joint Labour Committee in respect of their training, pay rates, certificates of training, hours of work, illness, lay-off etc. and the current position can be found in the Employment Regulation Order.

No cover

You are not covered by this Joint Labour Committee if you are involved in the making of any of the following:

❏ knitted or knitted fabric articles
❏ bonnets, caps (other than chef caps and hospital ward caps), gaiters, gloves, handkerchiefs, hats, mufflers, socks, spats, stockings
❏ boys' washing suits
❏ washable clothing worn by children
❏ any articles covered by the Trade Boards (Tailoring) Order 1919.

Overtime rates

Overtime rates are set out in the Employment Regulation Order and, at time of publication, are:

❏ hours in excess of thirty-nine – first four hours at time and a half, and from there on at double time
❏ hours on Sunday or prior to normal starting time on Monday – double time

❏ hours on a public holiday – double time plus a day off

The protection of Young Persons (Employment) Act applies.

Pay rates

Pay rates, piece rates and waiting time rates are contained in the Employment Regulation Order. The most up-to-date version can be obtained from the Joint Labour Committees Section of the Labour Court. The pay rates, at time of publication, for an adult working a basic thirty-nine hour week are:

❏ class 1 – £144.76
❏ class 2 – £144.02
❏ class 3 – £138.69
❏ class 4 – £128.76
❏ class 5 – £124.66

This ERO was issued in May 1994; the expected review date is May 1995.

Records

Records of the pay and hours of work of each employee covered by this Joint Labour Committee must be maintained for at least three years and be available for inspection (see 'Failure' above).

Service pay

This is provided for and is currently as follows:

❏ after five years – £0.50 per week
❏ after ten years – £1.00 per week
❏ after fifteen years – £1.50 per week
❏ after twenty years – £2.00 per week.

Type of operation

The work involved includes the making from textile fabrics of any or all of the following:

❏ men's aprons, chef caps, collars, cuffs, hospital ward caps, neckties, pyjamas, shirts or other washable clothing worn by males, and/or women's collars, cuffs, neckties and nurses' washing belts

❏ boxing, folding, laundering, smoothing, ornamenting, packing, warehousing, other operations normally associated with the making of the items specified above and any other connected duty.

TAILORING JOINT LABOUR COMMITTEE (JLC)

Purpose

To provide workers with basic *minimum* conditions of employment, such as pay, hours of work, overtime, holidays etc.

Who is covered

You are covered if you are employed anywhere in the state in any branch of the tailoring trade (see 'Job definitions', 'No cover' and 'Type' below).

DETAILS AND DEFINITIONS

Disputes

Disputes about any aspect of this Employment Regulation Order, including pay or conditions, can be dealt with directly by you, by your trade union, by the Joint Labour Committees Section of the Labour Court or by the Labour Inspectorate at the Department of Enterprise and Employment.

Employment Regulation Orders (EROs)

Employment Regulation Orders (EROs) are issued by the Joint Labour Committees following negotiation and agreement between trade unions and employers. They cover all aspects of your pay and conditions of employment and *must be displayed* in your workplace.

As aspects of the regulations, particularly pay rates, can vary from year to year, you should obtain a current Employment Regulation Order for your employment from:

Joint Labour Committees Section
The Labour Court
Tom Johnson House
Haddington Road
Dublin 4
Telephone (01) 660 8444

Failure or refusal

Failure or refusal on the part of the employer to:

❏ pay the rates set down, or
❏ comply with the conditions regarding hours, overtime rates, holidays etc., or
❏ maintain records for three years on each employee regarding pay, hours of work etc., or
❏ display the Employment Regulation Order can result in the employer having to compensate you for the loss suffered. In addition the employer can be fined up to £750 per offence.

Holidays

You are entitled to twenty days' annual leave per year plus nine public holidays, calculated in accordance with the Holiday (Employees) Act 1973.

Hours of work	Your hours of work are set at thirty-nine per week.
	The Protection of Young Persons (Employment) Act applies.
Job definitions	Job definitions or classes contained in the Employment Regulation Order are as follows:
Clothing branch	❏ measure cutter (Job Class 1) – someone who has sufficient skill to take a complete set of measures from model patterns and is capable of grading sizes
	❏ final inspector (Job Class 1) – someone who has responsibility for deciding the quality and standard of garments before dispatch
	❏ cutter or trimmer (Job Class 2) – someone employed wholly or mainly in one of the following processes: cutter, divider-of, fitter-up, layer-up, marker-in, waterproof maker
	❏ tailor (Job Class 2) – someone who, sewing by hand, alters, remakes, renovates, repairs a garment or portion of a garment
	❏ presser off (Job Class 2) – someone who has the necessary judgement and skill to press off garments to the required quality standard
	❏ various (Job Class 3) – someone who is employed as line passer, general worker, machine operator, packer, warehouse worker
	❏ machine operator (Job Class 4) – someone who is engaged full-time as relief and is skilled in a number of processes and machines
	❏ machine operator (Job Class 5) – someone who uses manual automatic or semi-automatic sewing processes in the making of a garment but who does not have the skills etc. of Classes 3 or 4 above

	❏ all other operations not covered in Job Classes 1, 2, 3, 4, and 5.
Hat making branch	❏ cutter (other than a lining cutter) (Job Class 1) – someone who is employed in cutting, marking in and using electric machine band knife sheers or hand knife ❏ blocker (Job Class 1) – someone who pulls-on or blocks hats or caps for shape making by the French gas block ❏ lining cutter (Job Class 2) – someone who is involved in cutting linings, interlinings, marking-out, laying or hooking-up ❏ warehouse worker (Job Class 2) – someone who is involved in stock keeping etc. ❏ packer (Job Class 3) – someone who is involved in the packing of goods and materials ❏ general workers (Job Class 3) – someone who performs operations requiring levels of skill in excess of Job Class 5 ❏ machine operator (Job Class 3) – someone who is full-time involved in sample making ❏ machine operator (Job Class 4) – someone who is employed full-time as relief and who has knowledge of a number of processes and machines ❏ machine operator (Job Class 5) – someone who uses manual automatic or semi-automatic sewing processes in the making of a garment but who does not have the skills etc. of Classes 3 or 4 above.
Learners	Learners are covered by this Joint Labour Committee in respect of their training, pay rates, certificates of training, hours of work, illness, lay-off etc. and the current position can be found in the Employment Regulation Order.

No cover

You are not covered by this Joint Labour Committee if you are involved in the making of any of the following:

❑ aprons
❑ knitted, oilskin, plastic or other rubberised headgear or headgear for boys and men where felting takes place in the same premises
❑ chef caps or similar
❑ boys' washing or sailing suits
❑ fur hats
❑ casting and making of solid metal helmets.

Overtime rates

Overtime rates can be found in the Employment Regulation Order and at time of publication were as follows:

❑ hours in excess of thirty-nine – first four hours at time and a half, and from there on at double time
❑ hours on a Sunday – double time
❑ hours on customary or public holidays – treble time or double time plus a day off.

Pay rates

Pay rates, piece rates and waiting time rates are contained in the Employment Regulation Order. The most up-to-date version can be obtained from the Joint Labour Committees Section of the Labour Court. The pay rates, at time of publication, for an adult working a basic thirty-nine hour week are:

❑ class 1 – £152.82
❑ class 2 – £149.67
❑ class 3 – £146.94
❑ class 4 – £133.59
❑ class 5 – £133.59

This ERO was issued in May 1994; the expected review date is May 1995.

Records

Records of the pay and hours of work of each employee covered by this Joint Labour Committee must be maintained for at least three years and be available for inspection (see 'Failure' above).

Service pay

Service pay is provided for and is currently as follows:

❏ after five years – £0.50 per week
❏ after ten years – £1.00 per week
❏ after fifteen years – £1.50 per week
❏ after twenty years – £2.00 per week.

Type of operation

The type of operation covered by this Joint Labour Committee includes any or all of the following:

❏ wholesale bespoke tailoring and retail bespoke tailoring (where it is for more than three retail establishments) for boys and men
❏ headgear for boys and men
❏ outer garments made from oilskin, plastic or any other rubberised material
❏ altering, assembling, cutting, cleaning, decorative needlework, dividing-off, embroidering, laundering, laying-up, marking-in, remaking, renovating, repairing, sewing, stock keeping, trimming, packing, warehousing, waterproofing and any other operations normally associated with the making of the items specified above.

WOMEN'S CLOTHING AND MILLINERY JOINT LABOUR COMMITTEE (JLC)

Purpose

To provide workers with basic *minimum* conditions of employment, such as pay, hours of work, overtime, holidays etc.

Who is covered

You are covered if you are employed anywhere in the state in any branch of the trade specified in either the Trade Boards (Women's Clothing and Millinery) Order 1926 or the Variation Order of 1944 (see 'Type' and 'No cover' below).

DETAILS AND DEFINITIONS

Disputes

Disputes about any aspect of this Employment Regulation Order, including pay or conditions, can be dealt with directly by you, by your trade union, by the Joint Labour Committees Section of the Labour Court or by the Labour Inspectorate at the Department of Enterprise and Employment.

Employment Regulation Orders (EROs)

Employment Regulation Orders (EROs) are issued by the Joint Labour Committees following negotiation and agreement between trade unions and employers. They cover all aspects of your pay and conditions of employment and *must be displayed* in your workplace.

As aspects of the regulations, particularly pay rates, can vary from year to year, you should obtain a current Employment Regulation Order for your employment from:

Joint Labour Committees Section
The Labour Court
Tom Johnson House
Haddington Road
Dublin 4
Telephone (01) 660 8444

Failure or refusal Failure or refusal on the part of the employer to:

❏ pay the rates set down, *or*
❏ comply with the conditions regarding hours, overtime rates, holidays etc., *or*
❏ maintain records for three years on each employee regarding pay, hours of work etc., *or*
❏ display the Employment Regulation Order

can result in the employer having to compensate you for the loss suffered. In addition the employer can be fined up to £750 per offence.

Holidays You are entitled to twenty days' annual leave per year plus nine public holidays, calculated in accordance with the Holiday (Employees) Act 1973.

Hours of work Your hours of work are set at thirty-nine per week.

The Protection of Young Persons (Employment) Act applies.

Five-day week A five-day week operates except with the agreement of both employer and employee.

Home worker A home worker is defined as a person who works in a place not under the control of the employer or company management, for example the worker's home.

Job definition

Job definitions of the various jobs covered by this Joint Labour Committee are set out here:

❏ measure cutter (Job Class 1) – someone who has the necessary skill to cut garments from patterns, take complete measurements and is capable of grading sizes etc.

❏ cutter or trimmer (Job Class 2) – someone who mostly works at cutting, trimming, marking-in or laying-up as well as the operations set out in Job Class 1 above

❏ tailor (Job Class 2) – someone who sews by hand in the process of making, altering, repairing, renovating or remaking a garment or a portion of a garment in a workroom or factory

❏ presser-off (Job Class 2) – someone who has the necessary skill to press-off a garment or a portion of a garment manually or by machine to the required quality standards

❏ (Job Class 3) – someone who has levels of skill and flexibility higher than that of Job Classes 4 and 5

❏ machine operator (Job Class 3) – someone full time on 'samples' or 'jumpers' when 'sample' work is not available

❏ machine operator (Job Class 4) – someone full time on float with the requisite skill on a variety of machines and operations

❏ machine operator (Job Class 5) – someone with less skill than those in Job Classes 3 and 4 whose duties are highly repetitive

❏ all other operations (Job Class 5) – someone not covered in Classes 1 to 5 inclusive.

Learners

Learners are covered by this Joint Labour Committee in respect of their training, pay rates, certificates of training, hours of work, illness, lay-off etc. and the current position can be found in the Employment Regulation Order.

No cover

You are not covered by this Joint Labour Committee if you are involved in any of the following:

❏ the making, packing or warehousing etc. of articles made from oilskin, plastic or rubberised materials, boots, collars and cuffs (women's), knitted articles or knitted fabric
❏ casting and making solid metal helmets, in lining with fur, when done in conjunction with the manufacture of furs, skin garments, rugs etc.
❏ branches of the trade covered by the Trade Board (Corset) Order 1919
❏ the making of hoods for women and children where the materials used are felted in the same premises.

Overtime

Overtime rates are contained in the Employment Regulation Order and at time of publication were as follows:

❏ first four hours – time and a half
❏ all hours after the first four hours – double time
❏ Sundays, public holidays and customary holidays – double time.

Pay rates

Pay rates including general minimum time-rate, home worker rates, incentive time-rate, learner rates, overtime rates and waiting time are all set out in the Employment Regulation Order. The most up-to-date version can be obtained from the Joint Labour Committees Section of the Labour Court. The pay rates, at time of publication, for an adult working a basic thirty-nine hour week are:

- class 1 – £151.69
- class 2 – £148.99
- class 3 – £144.97
- class 4 – £134.94
- class 5 – £133.61

This ERO was issued in May 1994; the expected review date is May 1995.

Records

Records of the pay and hours of work of each employee covered by this joint Labour Committee must be maintained for at least three years and be available for inspection (see 'Failure' above).

Service pay

Service pay is provided for and is currently as follows:

- after five years – £0.50 per week
- after ten years – £1.00 per week
- after fifteen years – £1.50 per week
- after twenty years – £2.00 per week.

Type of operation

The type of work covered by this Joint Labour Committee includes the making from knitted fabrics or textiles of any or all of the following:

- tailored and non-tailored clothes for women, girls or children
- boys' suits, the making of garments and headgear for women, girls and children
- altering, boxing, cleaning, cutting, decorative needlework, embroidery, folding, finishing, laundering, lining with fur, machine nickelling, machine paring, machine scalloping, machine thread-clipping, machine thread-drawing, machine top-sewing, making, ornamenting, packing, renovating or repairing (manually or by machine)

❏ smoothing or warehousing these items:
aprons, baby linen, blouses, blouse robes,
coats, coat frocks, costumes, dresses,
dressing gowns, dressing jackets, jumpers,
juvenile clothing, mantles, neckwear,
overalls, pyjamas, service clothing, skirts, tea
gowns, underclothing, underskirts, wraps or
similar articles.

Waiting time

Time must be paid at not less than the
appropriate rate as set out in the Employment
Regulation Order to any worker on the
company premises who is waiting for work
unless the employer can prove:

❏ the worker was on the premises without
permission
❏ the worker normally lived on the premises
❏ the worker was in a place normally used
for breaks, meals etc. where no work would
be performed.

USEFUL ADDRESSES

**Commission on the Status of
People with Disabilities**
Department of
Equality & Law Reform
43-49 Mespil Road, Dublin 4
Tel: 01-667 0344
Fax: 01-668 9933

**Construction Industry
Federation, The (CIF)**
Federation House, Canal Road
Dublin 6
Tel: 01-497 7487
Fax: 01-496 6953, 496 6611

**Council for the Status of
Women**
32 Upper Fitzwilliam Street
Dublin 2
Tel: 01-661 5268
Fax: 01-676 0860

Data Protection Commissioner
Block 4, Irish Life Centre
Talbot Street, Dublin 1
Tel: 01-874 8544
Fax: 01-874 5405

**Enterprise and Employment,
Department of**
65a Adelaide Road, Dublin 2
Tel: 01-676 5861
Fax: 01-676 9047

Employer-Labour Conference
65a Adelaide Road, Dublin 2
Tel: 01-676 4884

**Employment Appeals
Tribunal**
65a Adelaide Road, Dublin 2
Tel: 01-676 5861
Fax: 01-676 9047

**Employment Equality Agency
(EEA)**
36 Upper Mount Street, Dublin 2
Tel: 01-660 5966
Fax: 01-660 5813

**Equality and Law Reform
Department of**
43-49 Mespil Road, Dublin 4
Tel: 01-667 0344
Fax: 01-667 0366

Equality Officers
Tom Johnson House
Haddington Road, Dublin 4
Tel: 01-660 9662

FÁS
27-33 Upper Baggot Street
Dublin 4
Tel: 01-668 5777
Fax: 01-668 2691

**FLAC, Free Legal Advice
Centres Ltd**
49 South William Street, Dublin 2
Tel: 01-679 4239
Fax: 01-679 1554
Cork: CIC, Camden Quay, Cork

**Institute of Personnel
and Development**
35-39 Shelbourne Road, Dublin 4
Tel: 01-660 6644
Fax: 01-660 8030

Irish Business and Employers Confederation (IBEC)
Baggot Bridge House, 84-86
Lower Baggot Street, Dublin 2
Tel: 01-660 1011
Fax: 01-660 1717
Cork: Knockrea House
Douglas Road
    Tel: 021-362011
Mid-West: Gardner House
Bank Place, Charlotte's Quay
Limerick.
    Tel: 061 410411
North-West: 11 Main Street
Donegal
    Tel: 073-22474
South-East: 133 The Quay
Waterford
    Tel: 051-73855
West: Ross House
Victoria Place, Galway
    Tel: 091-61109

Irish Congress of Trade Unions (ICTU)
19 Raglan Road, Ballsbridge
Dublin 4
Tel: 01-668 0641
Fax: 01-660 9027

Irish National Organisation of the Unemployed
48 Fleet Street, Dublin 2
Tel: 01-679 5316
Fax: 01-679 2313

Joint Labour Committees Section
The Labour Court
Tom Johnson House
Haddington Road, Dublin 4
Tel: 01-660 8444

Labour Court
Tom Johnson House
Haddington Road, Dublin 4
Tel: 01-660 8444
Fax: 01-660 8437

Labour Relations Commission (LRC)
Tom Johnson House
Haddington Road, Dublin 4
Tel: 01-660 9662

Legal Aid Board
47 Upper Mount Street, Dublin 2
Tel: 01-661 5811
Fax: 01-676 3426
Athlone: Northgate Street
    Tel: 0902-74695
    Fax: 0902-72160
Castlebar: Humbert Mall
    Main Street.
    Tel: 094-24334
    Fax: 094-23721
Cork : 24 North Mall
    Tel: 021-300365
    Fax: 021-300307
1A South Mall
    Tel: 021-275998
    Fax: 021-276927
Dublin: 45 Lr Gardiner Street
    Tel: 01-878 7295
    Fax: 01-874 6896
9 Lower Ormond Quay
    Tel: 01-872 4133
    Fax: 01-872 4937
Aston House, Aston Place
    Tel: 01-671 2177
    Fax: 01-671 2336
517 Main Street, Tallaght
    Tel: 01-451 1519
    Fax: 01-451 7989

44-49 Main Street, Finglas
Tel: 01-864 0314
Fax: 01-864 0362
Dundalk: The Laurels
Tel: 042-30448
Fax: 042-30991
Galway: 5 Mary Street
Tel: 091-61650
Fax: 091-63825
Letterkenny: Houston House
Main Street
Tel: 074-26177
Fax: 074-26086
Limerick: Unit F, Lock Quay
Tel: 061-314599
Fax: 061-318330
Sligo: 1 Teeling Street
Tel: 071-61670
Fax: 071-61681
Tralee: 6 High Street
Tel: 066-26900
Fax: 066-23631
Waterford: 5 Catherine Street
Tel: 051- 55814
Fax: 051-71237

**Local Government Staff
Negotiations Board (LGSNB)**
Olaf House, 35-37 Ushers Quay
Dublin 8
Tel: 01-671 8400
Fax: 01-677 0023

**National Authority for
Occupational Safety & Health**
10 Hogan Place, Dublin 2
Tel: 01-662 0400
Fax: 01-662 0417

**National Irish Safety
Organisation**
Temple Court, 10 Hogan Place
Dublin 2
Tel: 01-662 0399
Fax: 01-662 0397

National Social Service Board
71 Lower Leeson Street, Dublin 2
Tel: 01-661 6422
Fax: 01-676 4908

Pensions Board, The
Holbrook House, Holles Street
Dublin 2
Tel: 01-676 2622
Fax: 01-676 4714

Rape Crisis Centre
70 Lower Leeson Street, Dublin 2
Tel: 01-661 4911
Fax: 01-661 0873

Rape Crisis Centre, Cork
26 MacCurtain Street, Cork
Tel: 021-968086

Revenue Commissioners
Dublin Castle, Dublin 2
Tel: 01-679 2777
Fax: 01-671 1826

Rights Commissioners
Tom Johnson House
Haddington Road, Dublin 4
Tel: 01-660 9662

Social Welfare, Department of
Áras Mhic Dhiarmada
Store Street, Dublin 1
Tel: 01-874 8444
Fax 01-704 3868

Centres for the Unemployed: Advice Centres

Leinster

Carlow Unemployed Centre
Forresters Hall
College Street, Carlow
Tel: 0503-32218

Noreside Unemployed Centre
22 Vicar Street, Kilkenny
Tel: 056-62146

Dundalk Resource Centre for the Unemployed
30 Clanbrassil Street
Dundalk, County Louth
Tel: 042-38820

Drogheda Resource Centre for the Unemployed
2 North Quay, Drogheda
County Louth
Tel: 041-35754

Dr Stevens Centre
Lloyds Lane, Athlone
County Westmeath
Tel: 0902-73001

Wexford Unemployed Centre
89 North Main Street
Wexford
Tel: 053-24482

Gorey Unemployed Information Centre
The Avenue, Gorey
County Wexford
Tel: 055-20037

New Ross Centre for the Unemployed
Roberts Street, New Ross
County Wexford
Tel: 051-22773

Little Bray Family Resource Centre
6 Ard Chualann, Bray
County Wicklow
Tel: 01-286 7644

St Fergal's Resource Centre
107 Old Court Avenue, Bray
County Wicklow
Tel: 01-282 5649

Wicklow Trade Union Centre for the Unemployed
'Madely', Florence Road, Bray
County Wicklow
Tel: 01-286 6730

Dublin
ABC
c/o Anne Devlin Resource Centre
Loreto Avenue, Rathfarnham
Dublin 14
Tel: 01-493 8320

Ballymun Jobs Centre
Unit 36, Ballymun Town Centre
Dublin 11
Tel: 01-842 5722

Ballymun Unemployed and Welfare Rights Centre
Sillogue Road, Ballymun
Dublin 11
Tel: 01-842 3244

Blakestown and Mountview Welfare Rights
Blakestown Resource Centre
Room 4, Blakestown, Dublin 15
Tel: 01-820 2270

Bohernabreena Community Enterprise
14 Allerton Drive
Tallaght, Dublin 24
Tel: 01-452 0685

Choices
Shanganagh Park House
Shankill, County Dublin
Tel: 01-282 0110

Connolly Centre
The Coombe, Dublin 8
Tel: 01-453 0803

Fingal Trade Union Centre for the Unemployed
St Helena's Resource Centre
St Helena's Road
Finglas South, Dublin 11
Tel: 01-834 5407

Free Legal Aid Centre
49 South William Street
Dublin 2
Tel: 01-679 4239/679 1554

Inner City Renewal Group
51 Amiens Street, Dublin 1
Tel: 01-874 4207

Irish Trade Union Trust (ITUT)
Solidarity House
48 Fleet Street
Dublin 2
Tel: 01-677 8294

Larkin Unemployed Centre
The North Strand, Dublin 3
Tel: 01-836 5544/836 5404

Loughlinstown Information Centre
56a Ennel Court
Loughlinstown
County Dublin
Tel: 01-282 1673

Mulhuddart Welfare Rights Group
Parslickstown House
Ladyswell Road, Mulhuddart
Dublin 15
Tel: 01-820 7327

NCCD Programme / Clondalkin Employment Development Centre
Rowlagh Community Centre
Clondalkin, Dublin 22
Tel: 01-457 0849

Northside Centre for the Unemployed
Glin Road, Bonnybrook
Dublin 17
Tel: 01-847 9463

Ringsend Action for Employment (RACE)
Thorncastle Community Centre
Thorncastle Street
Dublin 4
Tel: 01-660 7429

South Inner City Community Development Association (SICCDA)
90 Meath Street, Dublin 8
Tel: 01-454 0745/453 6098

Tallaght Welfare Society
1 Main Street, Tallaght
Dublin 24
Tel: 01-451 5911

West Tallaght Resource Centre
17 Glenshane Close
Tallaght, Dublin 24
Tel: 01-522 5333

Connaught
Centre for the Unemployed
Canavan House, Nuns Island
Galway
Tel: 091-64822

Castlebar Unemployed Centre
Hill House, Mountain View
Mayo
Tel: 094-22814
Centre for the Unemployed
Garden Street, Ballina
County Mayo
Tel: 096-70885

Sligo Unemployed Centre
The Village, High Street
Sligo
Tel: 071-42925

Munster
Community Resource Centre
Bantry, County Cork
Tel: 027-51315

Cork Council of Trade Unions Centre for the Unemployed
Exchange Buildings
34 Prince's Street, Cork
Tel: 021-275876

Clare Unemployed Resource Centre
Springfield House
Harmony Row, Ennis
County Clare
Tel: 065-41009

Dungarvan Resource Centre for the Unemployed
33 Lower Main Street
Dungarvan, County Waterford
Tel: 058-44099

Tralee Centre for the Unemployed
5 Whitestreet, Tralee
County Kerry
Tel: 066-27617

Limerick Centre for the Unemployed
33 Thomas Street, Limerick
Tel: 061-416090

Moyross Action Centre (PAUL)
Moyross Community Enterprise Centre,
Limerick
Tel: 061-455231

Our Lady of Lourdes
Greenfield Cross, Rosbrien
Limerick
Tel: 061-227830

PAUL (People Against Unemployment in Limerick)
Unit 25, The Tait Centre
Dominic Street, Limerick
Tel: 061-419388

Southill Action Centre
Southill House,
Roxboro Road, Limerick
Tel: 061-415340

Appendix

Code of Practice for the Employment of People with Disabilities in the Civil Service

Purpose

This Code of Practice is intended to support the civil service policy of equality of opportunity for people with disabilities.

Who is covered

All current or potential employees of the civil service.

'People with Disabilities' are defined in the code as people with physical, sensory, or psychological impairments which may:

❑ impact on their functional capability to do a particular job or to do it in a particular physical environment *or*
❑ be used against an individual in respect of obtaining or keeping a job which the person is otherwise capable of doing satisfactorily.

Accommodation and equipment

Your department will, in so far as practical, be obliged to ensure in a progressive way, the eradication of access or other such problems which impact on you. The department is also expected to adopt a positive approach to reasonable requests for equipment necessary for you to carry out your duties effectively.

Advice

Any query or request for assistance that cannot be dealt with by your immediate superior should be referred initially to the Equality Section, Department of Finance, (Agriculture House, Kildare Street, Dublin 2. Tel: 01–676 7571 ext. 3550)

Career development	Your manager is obliged, to the greatest extent possible, to treat you no less favourably than other employees in respect of the acquisition of skills, experience or training opportunities, staff mobility, interchanges, transfers etc.
Individual rights	You are entitled to have your case judged on its merits alone and not by reference to general assumptions about disabilities or previous practice.
Induction, integration	Your manager should be capable of discussing your disability in relation to the working environment in a frank, open and constructive fashion. Specifically, you can expect to be able to discuss the following:

❏ work location
❏ equipment
❏ any special difficulties
❏ the monitoring of your work and how any problems which may arise will be positively addressed.

Presumption of ability	You are entitled to expect that management and colleagues will presume your ability to carry out a task, unless otherwise demonstrated.
Promotion	Your manager will be obliged to positively encourage you towards promotion and an inability to carry out the full range of tasks of the higher graded position will not debar you from success.
Evacuation procedures	Any special requirements you have in order to safely evacuate your place of work should be made known to your safety officer. You are entitled to be *included* in any safety drill or procedure. Your manager is obliged to make your place of work safe in all respects.

GLOSSARY OF TERMS
AND ABBREVIATIONS

Actuarial evaluation

An assessment carried out to discover the financial health of a pension scheme fund.

Actuary

A person qualified to carry out an assessment of the financial health of a pensions scheme fund.

Additional voluntary contributions

A provision in many pension schemes which allows individuals to make additional voluntary contributions to the scheme where otherwise they would not have sufficient service to get a full pension.

Aggregate vote

The combined vote of the workers in a number of unions or branches of the same union.

Antenatal

Pertaining to the period of pregnancy before birth.

Arbitration

Binding decision from which there is no appeal.

Authorised trade union

A trade union which holds a current negotiating licence issued by the Minister for Enterprise and Employment.

AVCs

See additional voluntary contributions above.

Break of service

The termination of a contract of employment. It is sometimes used when the employer intends to re-employ the person or may break the service to prevent a person obtaining cover under the Unfair Dismissals Acts. A break of service can mean that previous service may not count when redundancy

	payments are being calculated.
Conciliation officer	An officer employed by the Labour Relations Commission to help resolve differences between trade unions and employers. The conciliation officer manages conciliation conferences.
Conciliation service	A service provided by the Labour Relations Commission, consisting of a conciliation officer and conciliation conferences. Its purpose is to help resolve disputes.
Constructive dismissal	The creation by an employer of conditions so intolerable that an employee feels compelled to resign from the employment.
Consultation procedure	A procedure which is used to allow either unions or employers to tell each other of proposed changes and to allow time for discussion before the changes are due for implementation, e.g. new work systems or a pay claim.
Continuity of service	This refers to the question of continuous employment or unbroken service and is used to calculate years of service for the purpose of deciding rights, benefits etc. in respect of notice, redundancy, unfair dismissal etc. Service prior to a break does not count when benefit or cover is being decided.
Continuous service	See Continuity of service above.
Deferred pension	Not availing oneself of a pension or a lump sum immediately but waiting until normal retirement age is reached.
Defined benefit	This describes the type of pension scheme where the benefit, i.e. pension, is defined but

	the contribution may vary.
Defined contribution	This describes the type of pension scheme where the contribution is defined but the benefit, i.e. pension, may vary.
Determination	A decision of the Labour Court or the Employment Appeals Tribunal, usually capable of being appealed only on a point of law.
Disciplinary procedure	A procedure set down in writing which describes how an employer will handle matters of discipline and the rights of the person being disciplined.
Disputes procedure	A procedure agreed between the employer and trade union on how they will handle disputes. It generally makes provision for the referral of disputes to third parties, such as the Labour Relations Commission conciliation service, Labour Court etc.
Domicile	A person's legally recognised place of residence.
EAT	See Employment Appeals Tribunal below.
EEA	See Employment Equality Agency below.
Employment agency	A private business seeking jobs for people or people for jobs.
Employment Appeals Tribunal (EAT)	A tribunal made up of three persons to hear cases in respect of unfair dismissal, redundancy, insolvency, minimum notice, part-time workers, payment of wages, maternity leave, contract information.
Employment Equality	The agency established to further the elimination of discrimination based on sex or

Agency (EEA) **Employment** **Regulation** **Order (ERO)**	marital status in all matters concerning work. This is issued by a Joint Labour Committee following negotiation and agreement between a trade union and an employer. It covers minimum rates of pay and conditions of employment in certain services or industries (see Part Two of this book).
Equality officer	An officer of the Labour Relations Commission who investigates and makes recommendations on cases of discrimination based on sex or marital status.
ERO	See Employment Regulation Order above.
Ex parte	An injunction granted at a hearing when only one of the parties to a dispute is present.
Fixed purpose contract	A contract intended for a particular job; the contract terminates when the job is finished.
Fixed term contract	A contract which terminates at a date set at the beginning of the employment.
Gender	The sex of an individual.
Grievance procedure	This is used to settle differences between employers and employees. It normally involves a number of steps before a full-time union official or an agency such as the Labour Relations Commission becomes involved.
Gross misconduct	This defines behaviour which may lead to instant dismissal. Such a dismissal does not however affect your rights under the Unfair Dismissals Acts.
Hearing	An investigation by the Labour Court, Employment Appeals Tribunal, Rights

	Commissioner etc.
Homeworker	A person covered by an Employment Regulation Order (see above) who works in the home.
IBEC	See Irish Business and Employers Confederation below.
ICTU	See Irish Congress of Trade Unions below.
Immunities	This is a term in general use to convey the fact that trade unions and their members involved in trade disputes (see below) cannot be sued by employers in certain circumstances.
Implementation	The carrying out of a decision of the Labour Court, Rights Commissioner etc.
Indirect discrimination	This takes place when an employer insists that an employee comply with an unnecessary condition of employment that, by and large, is more easily complied with by the opposite sex.
Industrial action	Action, such as strikes, aimed at forcing an employer to alter or maintain a contract of employment.
Injunction	In industrial relations terms a device used primarily by employers to prevent picketing. (See Ex parte above and Interlocutory below.)
Insolvency	Inability of an employer to meet financial obligations to an employee.
Interlocutory	An injunction granted where both parties to a dispute are present at a hearing held to decide an application.

Investigation	A word used to describe hearings (see above) of the Rights Commissioner, Labour Court, equality officer etc.
Irish Business and Employers Confederation	An organisation established and run by Irish employers to look after their interests. A body formed when the Federation of Irish Employers (FIE) and the Confederation of Irish Industry (CII) amalgamated.
Irish Congress of Trade Unions	The central authority for the trade union movement in Ireland with seventy unions affiliated.
JLC	See Joint Labour Committee below.
Job assessment	A comparative measure of one job as opposed to another (see Job evaluation below).
Job evaluation	A method of measuring the value of one job against another in terms of the physical and mental demands made on the employees concerned.
Joint industrial councils	These have been established by employers and trade unions to agree pay rates, conditions and procedures in such areas as construction, and state industrial employment. The agreements are legally binding when set out in a registered employment agreement (see below).
Joint Labour Committee	Established with the assistance of employers, trade unions and the Labour Court to set out legally binding pay rates and other conditions of employment in certain services, undertakings, trades or industries (see Part Two of this book). They issue Employment

Labour Court	Regulation Orders (see above). The court hears disputes between trade unions and employers and between employees and employers.
Labour Court recommendation	A decision of the Labour Court which is not legally binding on either party.
Labour Relations Commission	The commission provides a range of services to employees, trade unions and employers, to help resolve disputes.
LCR	See Labour Court recommendation above.
Lock-out	A form of industrial action taken by an employer in an attempt to force employees to either maintain or alter a contract of employment.
LRC	See Labour Relations Commission above.
Marital status	This describes whether or not you are married, single, separated, divorced etc.
Negotiation procedure	A procedure whereby trade unions and employers agree how they will process claims for pay, better conditions, changes in work practice etc.
Occupational schemes	Pension, savings, sick pay etc. are schemes covered by the use of the term 'Occupational'.
Outworker	A person employed but not working on premises owned or controlled by the management of a company.
Parties to the dispute	All the people who are in contention, e.g. employer, union, individual or group of workers.

Pay Related Social Insurance	A state deduction for social insurance benefits.
PAYE	**P**ay **A**s **Y**ou **E**arn refers to income tax automatically deducted by an employer on behalf of the Revenue Commissioners.
Payment in lieu	When the employer replaces benefits, e.g. holidays, notice, with a cash payment.
Period of notice	A set period of time which an employer is obliged to give to an employee before the termination of employment.
Positive discrimination	An act of positive discrimination is one aimed at addressing a gender imbalance, e.g. where there being substantially more men than women employed in a grade or category, an employer establishes a special training course for women. Positive discrimination is not unlawful.
Post-natal	Pertaining to the period after having given birth.
PR	See Proportional representation below.
Preserved benefit	When one does not avail oneself of a pension or a lump sum immediately but waits until normal retirement age is reached, one is said to preserve the benefit. Preserved benefits are governed by the Pensions Act.
Procedures	These are jointly agreed methods of processing problems at work.
Proportional Representation	A form of voting also used in elections to Dáil Éireann. It is intended to allow

(PR)	minorities to muster their votes as effectively as possible and to give parties a number of seats proportionate to the votes they win.
PRSI	See **P**ay **R**elated **S**ocial **I**nsurance above.
Quorum	The minimum number of people required to be in attendance for a meeting to be properly and legally taking place.
Reckonable service	The amount of days, weeks, months, years that can be included in the calculation of service with an employer in order to determine due notice and financial entitlement.
Recommendation	A decision of the Labour Court, Rights Commissioner, equality officer, which is not binding.
Redress	Compensation or remedy of an injustice.
Redundancy	Loss of a job through reorganisation, closure or partial closure of a company etc.
Registered employment agreements	Agreements, issued by joint industrial councils, which cover pay rates, conditions and procedures in areas like the construction industry and state industrial employment. Once registered with the Labour Court they become legally enforceable.
Redundancy Certificate	A certificate which must be issued to you by your employer if you become redundant.
Remuneration	Any reward received for work done.
Retrospection	Back pay.
Returning	The person in charge of an election.

officer

Right of appeal	In the event of a decision not being accepted the case can be heard again by a different person or group of persons by use of the 'right of appeal'.
Right of redress	See Redress above.
Rights Commissioner	An officer of the Labour Relations Commission who deals primarily with cases involving an individual. The Commissioner will also deal with issues arising under the Payment of Wages Act, the Unfair Dismissals Acts, the Terms of Employment (Information) Act and the Maternity (Protection of Employees) Act.
Secondary picketing	Picketing an employer other than your own in the course of a trade dispute.
Secret ballot	A decision taken using ballot papers and a ballot box instead of a show of hands. Decisions on industrial action *must* be taken by secret ballot.
Service certificate	A certificate setting out how long and in what category an employee was employed.
Statutory bodies	Organisations established with the involvement of the state usually having an Act of Dáil Éireann as part of their foundation.
Statutory instruments	Regulations made by a government minister as a result of power given to the minister by various Acts of Dáil Éireann.
Statutory redundancy	The minimum statutory payment; it is payable on loss of a job to a person with two or more years' service.

Submission	A written or verbal account of the case presented before the Labour Court, Rights Commissioner, equality officer etc.
Subpoena	A command to attend or make a submission to a tribunal.
Suspension	A form of disciplinary action in which an employee is instructed to leave the place of work either as a punishment or pending investigation. It may be with or without pay.
Terms of employment	The content of an employment contract including hours, pay, leave, pension etc.
Time limits	Deadlines which employees and employers must adhere to in exercising their rights.
Time off in lieu	Time usually granted by an employer to compensate for overtime worked which would normally attract payment of time and a half or double time.
TOIL	See Time off in lieu, above.
Trade disputes	Disputes, strikes, industrial action between employers and unions or employees and employers, but not between employees and employees.
Trust deed	Effectively the constitution or basic document of a pension scheme.
Trustees	The people with responsibility for the financial health of a pension scheme.
Union official	Usually a full-time employee of a trade union.

VEC	See Vocational Education Committee below.
VHI	See Voluntary Health Insurance below.
Vocational Education Committee	A statutory committee of a county council and certain other local authorities, established under the Vocational Education Act, 1930.
Voluntary Health Insurance	An insurance scheme which provides for health costs etc.
Waiting time	Periods of enforced idleness caused by delays in the work process owing to insufficient supply of material/product. These periods attract payment.

INDEX

A

address, employer's change of, 160
advertising
  and equal employment, 27-8
Aerated Waters and Wholesale
  Bottling JLC, 138, 140-3
  types of operation covered, 143
Agricultural Workers JLC, 138,
  144-8
  definitions, 144-5
alternative work
  and maternity leave, 59-60
annual leave. see holiday
  entitlement
Anti-Discrimination (Pay) Act
  1974, 13, 32, 51, 130
  details of, 17-21
  and employer insolvency, 83
appeals
  equal pay, 20
  against Rights Commissioner's
  decision, 53, 56
apprenticeship
  Catering JLC, 153
  Hairdressing (Cork) JLC, 165-6
  Hairdressing (Dublin & Dún
  Laoghaire) JLC, 170
  maternity leave, 60
  redundancy payments, 92
  unfair dismissal, 116
arbitration finding (Labour Court),
  52

B

Bacon Curing Council, 50
Bakery and Confectionery Trade
  Council, 50
ballots, secret, 56-7
bank holidays, 39
Banks Council, 50
beautician, definition of, 171
board and lodging
  Agricultural Workers JLC, 145
  Catering JLC, 153

board of directors
  worker representatives, 126-9
breaks
  Catering JLC, 153
  Hotels JLC, 178-9
  Retail Grocery & Allied Trades
  JLC, 191
Brush and Broom JLC, 138, 148-52
  types of operation covered, 152

C

catering establishment, definition
  of, 153
Catering JLC, 138, 152-9
  differentials, 154
  types of operation covered, 158-9
certificate of service
  Catering JLC, 153
  Hotels JLC, 179
  Retail Grocery & Allied Trades
  JLC, 191
  Contract Cleaning JLC, 160
change of hours, 160
change of ownership
  and continuity of employment,
  66
  and holiday entitlement, 37
  and maternity leave, 61
  and redundancy payments, 96
  and terms of employment, 110-
  11
  and unfair dismissal, 117
child, definition of, 88
church holidays, 37
Circuit Court, 8, 123
civil service
  equal employment, 28
codes of practice
  industrial relations, 42
collective agreements, 111
  and equal employment, 28
  and equal pay, 18
collective redundancies, 85-7
  ministerial intervention, 87

notification, 86
commission rates
    Hairdressing (Cork) JLC, 166
    Hairdressing (Dublin & Dún
    Laoghaire) JLC, 171
compassionate leave
    JLCs, 148, 171
compensation
    equal employment, 28-9
    unfair dismissal, 117
conciliation, 7
    conferences, 46-7
Construction Industry JIC, 50
constructive dismissal, 117-18
continuous service, 93
    rehiring, 100
    series of contracts, 123
    and transfer, 101
    unfair dismissal, 118
Contract Cleaning (City & County
    of Dublin) JLC, 139, 160-64
contract work
    unfair dismissal, 118-19
contractor, change of, 160
contracts
    changes to, 110-11
    content of, 112, 113
    Contract Cleaning JLC, 161
    description of, 66-7
    and equal employment, 29
    and equal pay, 18
    illegal, 120
    leaving work, 113
    part-time workers, 130
    powers of Minister, 113
    right to request, 113
    series of contracts, 123
    time limits, 114
    working abroad, 114-15
courts. see law courts
credit transfer, payment by, 72

D
death
    after notice of redundancy, 97
    and unfair dismissal claim, 119
deductions
    and employer insolvency, 84

defence forces
    equal employment, 27
    minimum notice, 65
    service in reserves, 93
    unfair dismissal, 116
determination
    Employment Appeals Tribunal, 70
    Labour Court, 52-3
differentials
    Catering JLC, 154
directors
    worker directors, 126-9
disciplinary action, warning of
    unfair dismissal, 125
disciplinary procedures. see
    individual JLCs
discrimination
    definition of, 29
    indirect, 32
    positive, 34
    unfair dismissal, 119
dismissal. see also unfair dismissal
    and equal pay claim, 18
disputes. see also under each JLC
    employer insolvency, 84
    holiday entitlement, 37-8
    part-time workers, 130
    payment of wages, 69
    procedures, 44-6
    redundancy payments, 97-8
District Court, 111
Dublin Wholesale Fruit and
    Vegetable Trade JIC, 50

E
Electrical Contracting Industry
    Council, 50
emergency services
    dispute procedures, 45
employee representatives
    duties and responsibilities, 42-4
employees
    safety and health obligations, 104
Employer Labour Conference
    description of, 9
employers
    change of address, 160
    death of, and redundancy, 98

definition of, 48
duties to employee
representatives, 42-4
inability to pay, 71
insolvency of, 82-5
proving unfair dismissal, 120-1
rebate on redundancy payments,
96, 98
restrictions on wage deductions,
73-4
safety and health obligations,
105, 106
employment, terms of. see terms of
employment
employment agencies
equal employment, 28
unfair dismissal, 120
Employment Agency Act 1971, 13
details of, 21-2
Employment Appeals Tribunal, 113
Acts under which claims heard,
13, 23
appeal against Rights
Commissioner's decision, 56
appeals from, 10
and codes of practice, 42
continuous service disputes, 94
description of, 8, 23-6
and employer insolvency, 84
maternity leave disputes, 61
part-time workers, 130
and payment of wages, 69-71
powers of, 26
terms of employment claims, 67,
109-10
unfair dismissal claims, 116-17,
118, 119, 120-1, 123
employment contract. see contracts
Employment Equality Act 1977,
13-14, 51, 130
details of, 26-36
and employer insolvency, 83
Employment Equality Agency, 18,
19
function of, 29-30
Employment Regulation Orders
(EROs), 9, 83, 137. see also
individual JLCs

Enterprise and Employment, Dept
of, 7, 83
appointment of LRC members, 53
authorised officers, 69
and codes of practice, 42
and Employment Appeals
Tribunal, 23-4
and Labour Court, 51
Labour Inspectorate, 9, 140
licences issued by, 22
notice of collective redundancies,
86-7, 100
powers over contents of contract,
113
Redundancy Payments Section,
95, 98
and terms of employment, 110
equal pay. see Anti-Discrimination
(Pay) Act 1974
equal work, 18-19
equality officers
role of, 8, 30-2, 33
essential services
dispute procedures, 45-6
European Union Pregnancy
Directive, 62, 122
exclusions
equal employment, 32
equal pay, 21

F
Factories Act 1955, 15, 106
fair dismissal, 120
favourable treatment
under Employment Equality Act
1977, 32
fees
employment agencies, 22
finishing time
Hotels JLC, 180
Flour Milling Council, 50
Footwear Industry JIC, 50
foreign employment, 120
foreign redundancy, 103

G
Garda Síochána
minimum notice, 65

occupational qualifications, 34
unfair dismissal, 116
goods and services
  as part of payment, 71
grievance, individual, 48
Grocery Provision and Allied
  Trades Council, 50

H
Hairdressing (Cork) JLC, 139, 165-9
  types of operation covered, 169
Hairdressing (Dublin and Dún
  Laoghaire) JLC, 139, 169-74
  types of operation covered, 174
hairdressing undertaking, definition
  of, 167
Handkerchief and Household Piece
  Goods JLC, 139, 174-8
  types of operation covered, 177-8
hat making
  Tailoring JLC, 202
health. see safety and health
High Court
  equal employment appeal, 31
  equal pay appeal, 20
  terms of employment disputes,
    110
Holiday (Employees) Acts 1973-91,
  14, 129, 130. see also individual
  JLCs
  details of, 36-40
holiday entitlement, 36. see also
  individual JLCs
  and jury duty, 58
  and maternity leave, 62
  minimum leave, 39
  part-time workers, 37, 130
  payment in lieu, 39
  timing of leave, 40
holiday pay, 38-9
home worker, definition of
  Women's Clothing & Millinery
    JLC, 206
Hosiery and Knitted Garments
  Manufacture Council, 50
hotel, definition of, 180-1
Hotels JLC, 139, 178-83
  extra responsibilities, 179-80

type of work covered, 183
hours of work. see also individual
  JLCs
  change of, 160
  unsocial hours, 194
  young persons, 88-9

I
immunity
  prosecution on trade disputes, 48
industrial action
  calculation of service, 67, 93, 100
  and continuous service, 93
  definition, 49
  picketing, 53-4
  procedures, 9
  secret ballots, 56-7
  and unfair dismissal, 123
  unofficial action, 57
industrial relations
  conciliation conferences, 46-7
  dispute procedures, 44-6
  immunity, 48
  individual grievance, 48
  worker v. worker disputes, 57
Industrial Relations Act 1969, 41,
  52, 53
Industrial Relations Act 1990, 14,
  53
  details of, 41-57
Industrial Relations Acts 1946,
  1969, 1976, 41
industrial relations procedures, 7-10
injunctions
  and industrial action, 49
Insolvency Act
  part-time workers, 130-1
insolvency of employer, 82-5, 130-1
inspection
  of employment agencies, 22
  safety and health, 107, 108
interviews
  equal employment, 32
Irish Business and Employers
  Confederation (IBEC)
  disputes in essential services, 46
  membership of Labour Court, 51
  membership of LRC, 53

Irish Congress of Trade Unions (ICTU), 23
  disputes in essential services, 46
  membership of Labour Court, 51
  membership of LRC, 53

J
job offers
  equal employment, 33
Joint Industrial Councils (JICs), 53
  description of, 8, 50
Joint Labour Committees (JLCs), 50, 53, 137-210
  description of, 8
  Employment Regulation Orders, 9
  function of, 137
  titles of, 138-9
Juries Act 1976, 14
  details of, 58-9

L
Labour Court
  appeal against Rights Commissioner's decision, 56
  appeals from, 10
  arbitration finding, 52
  codes of practice claims, 42
  description of, 9
  determination, 52-3
  dispute procedures, 44
  equal employment claims, 27-9, 30-1, 33
  equal pay claims, 20-1
  redundancy payments claims, 96
  role of, 50-1
  sexual harassment claims, 34
  unfair dismissal claims, 18, 121
Labour Inspectorate, 9
Labour Relations Commission
  codes of practice, 42
  conciliation conferences, 46-7
  description of, 7-8
  dispute procedures, 44
  disputes in essential services, 46
  equal employment claims, 30
  equal pay claims, 17, 19-20
  and JICs, 50

  and Labour Court, 51
  redundancy payments claims, 96
  role of, 53
  unfair dismissal claims, 121
Law Clerks JLC, 139, 183-6
  types of worker covered, 186
law courts
  description of, 10
  unfair dismissal, 121, 123
  unlawful deductions, 71-2
lay-offs, 100
learners
  Handkerchief & Household Piece Goods JLC, 176
  Shirtmaking JLC, 197
  Tailoring JLC, 202
  Women's Clothing & Millinery JLC, 207-8
leave. see holiday entitlement; maternity leave; sick leave
legislative acts, 13-133
  summary of, 13-16
length of service. see service, length of
licences
  employment agencies, 22
Licensing Acts 1833-1962, 181
'like work', 18-19
Local Appointments Commissioners
  equal employment, 28
lock-outs, 121
  and length of service, 68, 93, 100
  unfair dismissal, 123
lump sums
  redundancy payments, 95-6

M
manicurist, definition of, 167, 173
marital status
  and equal employment, 33
maternity leave
  basic, 61
  and continuous service, 93
  extra, 61
  notice of, 62-3
  part-time workers, 131
  premature birth, 64

236

and redundancy notice, 100
still birth or miscarriage, 60, 61
and unfair dismissal, 122
Maternity (Protection of
Employees) Acts 1981, 1991, 13,
14, 23, 93, 129
details of, 59-64
Merchant Shipping Act, 65
minimum leave, 38
minimum notice, 65-8
part-time workers, 131-2
Minimum Notice and Terms of
Employment Acts 1973-91, 13,
14, 23, 73-4, 83, 92, 129, 131-2
details of, 65-8
miscarriage
and maternity leave, 61
misconduct
and termination of contract, 67

N

National Authority for Occupational
Safety and Health, 15, 103, 104-5
night work
Hotels JLC, 181
young persons, 89
notice. see minimum notice

O

obstruction
of equality officer, 33
occupational qualifications
and equal employment, 33-4
overtime. see also individual JLCs
calculation of pay, 102
young persons, 90
ownership. see change of ownership

P

part-time workers, 129-33
Catering JLC, 156-7
contracts, 130
holiday entitlement, 37, 130
Insolvency Act, 130-1
maternity leave, 131
minimum notice, 131-2
notice of termination, 132
re-hired, 133

reduction of hours, 132-3
redundancy, 133
unfair dismissal, 133
pay, definition of, 21
pay, holiday, 38-9
pay rates. see individual JLCs
payment of wages
inability to pay, 71
and jury duty, 58
loss due to employer insolvency,
84
pay slip, 72
payment systems, 73
receipts, 73
reduction of young person's
wages, 90
restrictions on deductions, 73-4
time limit on complaints, 74
valid deductions, 75
week's pay, definition of, 102
Payment of Wages Act 1991, 13,
14-15, 23, 55, 130
details of, 68-75
pension schemes
and employer insolvency, 85
investigations, 80
leaving work, 80
minimum funding, 80
refund of contributions, 80-1
trust deeds, 81
vested rights, 81
pensions. see individual JLCs
Pensions Act 1990, 15, 76-81
Pensions Board, 15, 76, 80
picketing, 53-4
piece workers
week's pay, 102
positive discrimination, 34
pregnancy. see also maternity leave
favourable treatment in, 32, 34
and unfair dismissal, 118, 122
Printing and Allied Trades in
Dublin Council, 50
prison service
occupational qualifications, 34
probation
and maternity leave, 60
and unfair dismissal, 122

Protection of Employees
(Employers' Insolvency) Acts
1984-91, 13, 15, 23, 129
details of, 82-5
Protection of Employment Act
1977, 15
details of, 85-7
Protection of Young Persons
(Employment) Act 1977, 15. see
also under individual JLCs
details of, 87-90
Provender Milling JLC, 139, 187-
90
type of work covered, 190
pub, definition of, 153
public holidays, 37
definition and entitlement, 39-40

Q
qualifications, occupational
and equal employment, 33-4

R
reckonable service, 94-5
records. see under individual JLCs
reduction of hours
part-time workers, 132-3
redundancy
collective, 85-7
death after redundancy notice, 97
definition of, 97
and equal employment, 29
failure to notify, 98
foreign, 103
notice of, 99-100
part-time workers, 133
time off to seek work, 101
and unfair dismissal, 123
unfair selection, 101
redundancy payments
alternative work, 91-2
calculation of, 92-6
failure to pay, 98-9
leaving before expiry of notice, 99
tax and social welfare, 101
voluntary redundancy, 97
working abroad, 102
Redundancy Payments Acts 1967-91,
13, 15, 23, 129
details of, 91-103
and employer insolvency, 82
registered employment agreements,
54, 146-7
Retail Grocery and Allied Trades
JLC, 139, 190-4
extra responsibility, 192
types of work covered, 194
unsocial hours, 194
Revenue Commissioners, 120, 164
Rights Commissioners, 24, 114
appeal against decision by, 53
and conciliation, 47
maternity leave disputes, 61
and payment of wages, 69-71, 74
role of, 8, 54-6
terms of employment disputes,
109-10, 111, 113
unfair dismissal claims, 116, 118,
119, 120-1, 123, 125

S
Safety, Health and Welfare at Work
Act 1989, 15, 130
details of, 103-5
safety and health
powers of safety representatives,
104-5
in pregnancy, 62
safety committees, 106-8
safety delegate, 108
safety statements, 105, 108-9
Safety in Industry Act 1980, 15
details of, 106-9
secondary picketing, 54
secret ballots, 56-7
self-employed
safety and health obligations, 105
service, length of. see also
certificate of service;
continuous service
and jury duty, 59
notice entitlement, 67
reckonable service, 94-5
and strikes, 68
and unfair dismissal, 117, 118
service pay. see individual JLCs

sexual harassment, definition of, 34-5
shift workers
  week's pay, 102
Shirtmaking JLC, 139, 194-9
  job definition, 196-7
  types of operation covered, 198-9
short time working, 100
sick leave
  and holiday entitlement, 40
  and maternity leave, 64
sick pay
  Brush and Broom JLC, 151
  Hairdressing (Dublin & Dún Laoghaire) JLC, 174
  Provender Milling JLC, 190
Social Insurance Fund, 82, 85
  redundancy payments, 98-9
Social Welfare, Department of, 120, 164
  maternity leave payment, 63
social welfare benefit
  and redundancy payments, 101
spread-over duty
  Catering JLC, 158
  Hotels JLC, 182-3
state enterprises
  worker directors, 126-9
State Industrial Employees Council, 50
still birth
  and maternity leave, 60
strike action
  procedures, 9
strikes. see industrial action
Succession Act 1965, 83
Sunday leave
  Catering JLC, 158
Sunday work
  Contract Cleaning JLC, 164

T
Tailoring JLC, 139, 199-204
  job definitions, 201-2
  types of operation covered, 204
taxation
  of redundancy payments, 101
Telecom Council, 50

termination, notice of, 132
terms of employment, 68
  change of contract, 110-11
  content of contract, 112
  leaving work, 113
Terms of Employment (Information) Act 1994, 13, 16, 23, 55, 65, 66, 68, 132
  covers part-time workers, 130
  details of, 109-15
  written terms obligatory, 73-4
time limits
  employment contracts, 114
  equal employment, 35
  unfair dismissal, 123-4
Trade Board (Corset) Order 1919, 208
Trade Board (Handkerchief and Household Goods) Order 1935, 175
Trade Boards (Shirtmaking) Order 1920, 194
Trade Boards (Tailoring) Order 1919, 197
Trade Boards (Women's Clothing and Millinery) Order 1926, 205
trade dispute, definition of, 57
trade disputes. see industrial action
Trade Disputes Act 1906, 41
Trade Disputes Amendment Act 1982, 41
Trade Union Acts 1941, 1971, 41
trade unions. see also employee representatives
  contributions to, 164
  equal opportunity, 36
  immunity, 48
  rules, 57
  secret ballots, 56-7
  union activity and unfair dismissal, 118, 124
training
  equal opportunity, 35-6
  and maternity leave, 60
travel allowance
  Contract Cleaning JLC, 164
trust deeds, 81

trustees
  pensions, 77-9, 81

U
unfair dismissal
  appeals, 116-17
  compensation, 117
  constructive dismissal, 117-18
  and continuous service, 93
  contract work, 118-19
  definition of, 124-5
  disciplinary procedures, 119
  disputes, 119
  and employment agency, 22
  equal employment claim, 29
  equal pay claim, 18
  foreign contracts, 120
  illegal contracts, 120
  immediate dismissal, 121
  and maternity leave, 61
  obstruction of tribunal, 121
  part-time workers, 133
  persons not covered, 115-16
  and pregnancy, 122
  and probation, 122
  re-employment, 123
  and redundancy, 123
  time limit on claim, 123-4
  and trade union activity, 124
  unfair selection for redundancy,
    101
Unfair Dismissals Acts 1977-93, 13,
  16, 23, 55, 61, 66, 110, 129, 133
  details of, 115-25
  and employer insolvency, 82-3
Unfair Dismissals Amendment Act
  1993, 22, 120
unions. see trade unions
unofficial action, 57

V
Variation Order 1944, 205
victimisation
  and Employment Equality Act
    1977, 36
voluntary redundancy, 97

W
wages. see payment of wages
  definition of, 21, 75
waiting time
  Women's Clothing & Millinery
    JLC, 210
warning of disciplinary action, 125
week's pay, definition of, 102
welfare. see safety and health;
  social welfare
Women's Clothing and Millinery
  JLC, 139, 205-10
  job definition, 207
  types of operation covered, 209-
    10
Woollen and Worsted Manufacture
  Council, 50
worker, definition of, 57
worker directors, 126-9
  part-time workers, 132
Worker Participation (State
  Enterprises) Acts 1977-93, 16,
  129
  details of, 126-9
Worker Protection (Regular Part-
  Time Employees) Act 1991, 13,
  16, 23, 37, 162
  details of, 129-33
working abroad
  foreign contracts, 120
  redundancy, 102, 103
  terms of employment, 114-15

Y
young persons
  definition of, 90
  maximum hours of work, 88-9
  night work, 89
  overtime, 90
  protection of, 87-90